How to Start & Manage a Garden Center Business

A Practical Way to Start Your Own Business

By
Jerre G. Lewis and Leslie D. Renn

How to Start & Manage
A Garden Center Business

Lewis & Renn Associates, Inc.

Business & Professional Publishing

10315 Harmony Drive
Interlochen, Michigan 49643
(231) 275-7287

Leslie D. Renn
President

Jerre G. Lewis
Secretary-Treasurer

ISBN # 978-1-57916-154-5
Library of Congress Catalog Card Number
99-094191

TABLE OF CONTENTS

Chapter 1

Introduction

Selecting the right Garden Center business opportunity requires careful, thorough evaluations of yourself. Owning your own business is as much a part of the American dream as owning a home, and for you, this urge represents one of life's most exciting challenges. This book is for those men and women who someday may go into business for themselves and for those who are already in business for themselves but wish to strengthen their entrepreneurial and managerial skills.

Entrepreneurs come in all shapes and sizes, personalities, and lifestyles. They are usually highly motivated, hard-working individuals who receive satisfaction from taking risks. Your business should interest you, not just be an income generator. Analyze your personal style. Do you like working with people? Are you a self starter, goal oriented, persistent, a risk taker, willing to work hard and long hours?

If you have been honest in evaluating yourself, you will now select the right type of business. Before you can determine which of the multitude of businesses is right for you to start, you must evaluate the businesses you want to start by asking these questions. Is the business area growing? How does the economy affect it? Who dominates its market? Once you have considered a business that satisfies your needs and interest you must prepare a formal business plan by following the outline given in this book.

Small businesses constitute a dynamic and critical sector of the U.S. economy. Every year in the United States more than 600,000 new businesses are launched by independent men and women eager to make their own decisions, express their own ideas, and be their own bosses. But running your own business is not as easy as it may seem. There can be problems with the inventory, or getting the right goods delivered on time. Yet, managing one's own business can be a personally and financially rewarding experience for an individual strong enough to meet the test. A person with stamina, maturity, and creativity, one who is willing to make sacrifices, may find making a go of a struggling enterprise an exhilarating challenge with many compensations.

Small business owners are a dedicated group of people who work hard and whose hours on the job usually exceed the nine-to-five routine. The owner's commitment is the key to many successful small businesses; an entrepreneur is able to communicate ideas, lead, plan, be patient, and work well with people.

Managing a business requires more than the possession of technical knowledge. Because most small businesses are started by technical people, such as engineers and salesmen, their managerial acumen is often less developed than their technical skills. The need to plan for management is common to every type of and size of business, and there are certain steps that must be taken. Although some of them are very elementary — such as applying for a city business permit — the most important are often complex and difficult and require the advice of specialists: accountants, attorneys, insurance brokers, and/or bankers. For almost any business though, the first step will be to translate the entrepreneur's basic idea into a concrete plan for action.

To gauge your level of entrepreneurial spirit, the following quiz was created. Please answer each question honestly and then total the columns.

ENTREPRENEURIAL QUIZ

	YES	NO	SOMETIMES
1. I am a self-starter. Nobody has to tell me how to get going.	____	____	_____
2. I am capable of getting along with just about everybody.	____	____	_____
3. I have no trouble getting people to follow my lead.	____	____	_____
4. I like to be in charge of things and see them through.	____	____	_____
5. I always plan ahead before beginning a project. I am usually the one who gets everyone organized.	____	____	_____
6. I have a lot of stamina. I can keep going as long as necessary.	____	____	_____
7. I have no trouble making decisions and can make up my mind in a hurry.	____	____	_____
8. I say exactly what I mean. People can trust me.	____	____	_____
9. Once I make my mind up to do something, nothing can stop me.	____	____	_____
10. I am in excellent health and have a lot of energy.	____	____	_____

	YES	NO	SOMETIMES

11. I have experience or technical knowledge in the business I intend to start. ___ ___ ___

12. I feel comfortable taking risks if it is something I really believe in. ___ ___ ___

13. I have good communication skills. ___ ___ ___

14. I am flexible in my dealings with people and situations. ___ ___ ___

15. I consider myself creative and resourceful. ___ ___ ___

16. I can analyze a situation and take steps to correct problems. ___ ___ ___

17. I think I am capable of maintaining a good working relationship with employees. ___ ___ ___

18. I am not a dictator. I am willing to listen to employees, customers and suppliers. ___ ___ ___

19. I am not rigid in my policies. I am willing to adjust to meet the needs of employees, customers, and suppliers. ___ ___ ___

20. More than anything else, I want to run my own business. ___ ___ ___

Total of Column #1 _____

Total of Column #2 _____

Total of Column #3 _____

If the total of Column #1 is the highest, then you will probably be very successful in running your own business.

If the total of Column #2 is the highest, you may find that running a business is more than you can handle.

If the total of Column #3 is the highest, you should consider taking on a partner who is strong in your weak areas.

NOTE: This quiz was adapted from the Small Business Administration publication *Checklist for Going Into Business.*

Notes _____

Chapter 2

Planning the Business

The Dream of self-employment can be fulfilled. You don't need to finance the opening of an elaborate office or facility to start your own one-person corporation either. You can start your own Garden Center business.

Anyone preparing to run an Garden Center business needs to learn a great deal to assure the best possible chance for success.

GETTING STARTED

The following is a list of what you need to accomplish to insure that your Garden Center endeavor will head in the right direction.

1. Define your educational background and work experience.

2. Survey all the basic types of Garden Center businesses.

3. Define what products or services your Garden Center business will be marketing.

4. Define who will be using your products/services.

5. Define why they will be purchasing your products/services.

6. List all competitors in your Garden Center marketing area.

ZONING REGISTRATIONS

Garden Center businesses are subject to many laws and regulations enforced by state, county, township governmental units. Most jurisdictions now have codes, a zoning board, and an appeal board which regulate businesses. Areas often are zoned residential, commercial or industrial.

You must become familiar with these regulations. If you are doing business in violation of these regulations, you could be issued a cease and desist order or fined.

Certain kinds of goods cannot be produced in the home, though these restrictions vary somewhat from state-to-state. Most states outlaw home production of fireworks, drugs, poisons, explosives, sanitary/medical products and some toys.

Many localities have registration requirements for new businesses. You will need to obtain a work certificate or license from the state.

TAX REQUIREMENTS

<u>Application for Employer Identification Number</u>, Form SS-4. This registers you with the Internal Revenue Service as a business. If you have employees, you should ask for Circular E along with your ID number. Circular E explains federal income and social security tax withholding requirements.

<u>Employer's Annual Unemployment Tax Return</u>, Form 940. This is only if you have employees. It's used to report and pay the Federal Unemployment Compensation Tax.

<u>Employee's Withholding Allowance Certificate</u>, W-4. Every employee must complete the W-4 so the proper amount of income tax can be withheld from the

employee's pay. If the employee claims more than 15 allowances or a complete withholding exemption while having a salary of more than $200 a week, a copy of the W-4 must go to the IRS.

Employer's Wage and Tax Statement, W-2. Used to report to the IRS the total taxes withheld and total compensation paid to each employee per year.

Reconciliation/Transmittal of Income and Tax Statements, W-3. Used to total all information from the W-2. Sent to the Social Security Administration.

The IRS puts on monthly workshops on understanding and using these forms. Call your local IRS office for further information.

States also have various tax form requirements including: an unemployment tax form, a certificate of registration application, a sales and use tax return, an employer's quarterly contribution and payroll report, an income tax withholding registration form, an income tax withholding form, and others. Some forms apply only to employers who have employees. Your local IRS office and state Office of Taxation can provide you with listings of forms you will need to start your business. The following table outlines Federal tax form requirements.

Every small business begins with an idea — a product to be manufactured or sold, a service to be performed.

Whatever the business or its degree of complexity, the owner needs a business plan in order to transform a vision into a working operation.

This business plan should describe in writing and in figures the proposed Garden Center business and its products, services, or manufacturing processes. It should also include an analysis of the market, a marketing strategy, an organizational plan, and measurable financial objectives.

WHAT SHOULD A BUSINESS PLAN COVER?

It should be a thorough and objective analysis of both personal abilities and business requirements for a particular product or service. It should define strategies for such functions as marketing and production, organization and legal aspects, accounting and finance. A business plan should answer such questions as:

What do I want and what am I capable of doing?

What are the most workable ways of achieving my goals?

What can I expect in the future?

There is no single best way to begin. What follows is simply a guide and can be changed to suit individual needs.

1. Define Long-term goals.
2. State short-term.
3. Set marketing strategies to meet goals and objectives.
4. Analyze available resources.
5. Assemble financial data.
6. Review plan.

Please refer to Figure 2.1 for a complete business plan outline.

The business operator with a realistic plan has the best chance for success.

Figure 2.1

BUSINESS PLAN FOR SMALL BUSINESSES

    I.   Type of Business

   II.   Location

  III.   Target Market

  IV.   Planning Process

    V.   Organizational Structure

  VI.   Staffing Procedures

 VII.   Market Strategy

  IX.   Financial Planning

    X.   Budgeted Balance Sheet

  XI.   Budgeted Income Statement

 XII.   Budgeted Cash Flow Statement

XIII.   Break-Even Chart

Notes _____

Chapter 3

Marketing Strategies
for an Garden Center Business

As a potential Garden Center business owner, it is important to learn all you can about marketing. You will need to know how to identify your market and how to market your product or service.

As a business person who looks for a profit from the sale of goods, you recognize that without people who want to buy, there is no demand for the things you want to sell. Thus, it is important that, in addition to knowing about the functions of marketing, you also study the activities that will influence the consumer. When you satisfy the specific needs and wants of the customer, then he or she may be willing to pay you a price that will include a profit for you — and to make a profit is one of the reasons you have become an Garden Center business owner. Although there are many activities connected with marketing, most of them can be classified in these categories: buy, finance, transport, standardize, store, insure, advertise and sell.

Target Market Analysis

Before you can create a successful marketing campaign, it's necessary to determine your target market (toward whom to direct your energies). The whole concept of target marketing can seem very scary at first. On the surface, targeting appears to be limiting the scope of the pool of potential customers. Many people fear that by defining a market, they will lose business. They are concerned that they will choose the wrong market. Or that other practitioners will take just anybody and therefore some of their business.

You must keep in mind that the purpose of defining your target market is to make your life easier and increase the productivity of your promotional endeavors. Many opportunities exist in this world and it's impossible to pursue them all or be everything to everyone. You need to know where to focus your energy and money when it comes to promotion and advertising.

The two most common means of market analysis are demographics and psychographics, which describe a person in terms of objective data and personality attributes.

Demographics are statistics such as:
- age
- gender
- income level
- geographic location
- occupation
- education level

Psychographics are lifestyle factors including:
- special interest activities
- philosophical beliefs
- social factors
- cultural involvements

The more you know about your potential customers, the easier it is to develop an appropriate position statement and design an effective marketing campaign. The actual number of target markets you have depends mainly upon the size of your practice and the scope of your knowledge.

Your Target Market Profile

In order to clarify your target market(s) you need to delineate the demographic and psychographic factors and then identify the characteristics your customers have in common.

Describe your current customers and those who are most likely your future customers:

What is the age range and average age of your customers?

What is the percentage of males?

What is the percentage of females?

What is the average educational level of your customers?

Where do your customers live?

What are the occupations of your customers?

Where do your customers work?

What is the average annual income level of your customers?

Of what special interest groups are your customers members?

What is the primary reason your customers use your services?

Defining Your Target Market(s)

Write a descriptive statement for each of your target markets (refer to your "Target Market Profile"). Include a brief overview of the services you are providing to that group and a detailed analysis of the characteristics of the specific clientele.

Target Market 1:

Target Market 2:

Target Market 3:

Garden Center Business Marketing

The foundation for creating a thriving customer base.

A. Overview

This section is about clarifying your beliefs and attitudes toward your profession and determining the image you wish to portray.

1. Describe the "character" that you want for your business. Depict the image you want to convey:

2. State your philosophy in regard to your business:

3. Describe your philosophy regarding your practice in business:

B. Customer Profile

This is a descriptive analysis of your current and potential customers — who they are, what their interests are, and where you can find them. Include each of your target markets.

1. Target Market 1:

2. Target Market 2:

3. Target Market 3:

C. Competition's Marketing Assessment

The first phase in planning your promotional campaign is appraising the competition. List each of your major competitors and describe the marketing strategies they utilize. Be certain to include where and how often they advertise.

1. Major Competitor 1:

2. Major Competitor 2:

3. Major Competitor 3:

4. Major Competitor 4:

5. Major Competitor 5:

6. Major Competitor 6:

Garden Center Marketing Planning

Outline for Marketing:

I. Produce/Service Concept
    A. Name of produce or service
    B. Descriptive characteristics of product or service
    C. Unit sales
    D. Analysis of market trends

II. Number of Customers in Market Area:
    A. Profile of customers
    B. Average customer expenditure
    C. Total market

III. Your Market Potential:
    A. Total market divided by competition
    B. Total market multiplied by percent who will buy your product

IV. Needs of Customers:
    A. Identification
    B. Pleasure
    C. Social approval
    D. Personal interest
    E. Price

V. Direct Marketing Sources:
    A. Trade magazines
    B. Trade associates
    C. Small Business Administration (SBA)
    D. Government publications
    E. Yellow Pages
    F. Marketing directories

VI. Customer Profile:
    A. Geographical
    B. Gender
    C. Age range
    D. Income brackets
    E. Occupation
    F. Educational level

Chapter 4

Promoting the Garden Center Business

When a new business is opened, the owner must be prepared to publicize the business or its chance for success will be slim. Only a few businesses — such as those with a prime location, nationally known name, or a built-in clientele — can succeed without advertising to promote market awareness and stimulate sales.

The first purpose — promoting customer awareness — applies as much to established businesses as to newcomers.

In the Garden Center business, you will find it easier to retain old customers than to win new ones. When old customers move away from your area, or when their buying needs change, you need new customers to maintain your sales volume. If you expect your business to gain, you will need additional new customers. New customers are those who move into your area or who have grown into your line of products because now they can afford them or they need them. We see advertising and we hear advertising all around us, and yet that is only a part of it. Through advertising, you call the attention of customers to your products.

As a small business owner, you may advertise your business through your location. People pass by and are attracted to your operation because of what you are selling. To get a better idea of what advertising is, consider some of the following functions of advertising:

1. *To inform:* Letting customers know what you have for sale through brochures, leaflets, newspapers, radio, TV, and etc.

2. *Persuade:* Persuasion is the art of leading individuals to do what you want them to do. There are sales personnel who have persuasive sales presentations, but persuasion in advertising is nonpersonal. The appeal is made through the printed or spoken words or a picture. The influence of an ad on readers occurs as purchasers choose what they want among different products, and different wants. To gain the actions you want — a sale — you must persuade a customer to examine personally what you have for sale.

3. *Reminder:* Advertising performs it's third function when it reminds those who have been persuaded to buy once that the same product will bring satisfaction. The ad will also remind a customer of the characteristics of a product purchased some time ago, and where he or she bought it. Because customers change their loyalty to a place of business, their taste for products, and often their trading area patronage, advertising is necessary to draw new customers and to hold old customers. To generate results from advertising that will be profitable to your business, you will have to produce answers to the what, where and how of advertising.

What to Advertise

The nature of your business will partially answer the question "Shall I advertise goods or services?" What are the outstanding features of your business? Is it unique in any way? Does it have strong points? Do you have something to offer that the competition is not able to duplicate? Answers to these questions will give you a start in deciding what to advertise.

Where to Advertise

Of course, you will want to advertise within your marketing area, however there are a few guidelines to remember:

A. Who are your customers?

B. What is their income range?

C. Why do they buy?

D. How do they buy? Do they pay Cash? Charge?

E. What is the radius of your market area?

How to Advertise:

In determining how to advertise, you will have to consider your dollar allocation for advertising and the media suitable to your particular kind of business. However, it is important to have a balance between the presentation of the product or service being advertised and the application of three basic principles.

1. Gain the attention of the audience.

2. Establish a need.

3. Tell where that need may be filled.

See Figure A for an outline of the different advertising media and Figure B for budget on media goals.

Advertising Media

Media	Market Coverage	Type of Audience
Daily Newspaper	Single community or entire metro area; zoned editions sometimes available	General
Weekly Newspaper	Single community	Residents
Telephone Directory	Geographical area or occupational field served by the directory	Active shoppers for goods or services
Direct mail audience	Controlled by the advertiser	Controlled
Radio audience	Definable market area	Selected
Television audience	Definable market area	Various
Outdoor	Entire metro area	General auto drivers
Magazine	Entire metro area or magazine region	Selected audience

Figure A

Promotion and Advertising Plan — Garden Center Business

In designing your promotional plan, it's wise to use a variety of media. You must have specific goals, time lines and budgets for each marketing application

Media	Goal	Timeline	Budget

Notes _____

Chapter 5

Financial Planning for an Garden Center Business

Financial planning is the process of analyzing and monitoring the financial performance of your business so you can assess your current position and anticipate future problem areas. The daily, monthly, seasonal, and yearly operation of your business requires attention to the figures that tell you about the firm's financial health.

Maintaining good financial records is a necessary part of doing business.

The increasing number of governmental regulations alone makes it virtually impossible to avoid keeping detailed records. Just as important is to keep them for yourself. The success of your business depends on them. An efficient system of record keeping can help you to:

- make management decisions
- compete in the marketplace
- monitor performance
- keep track of expenses
- eliminate unprofitable merchandise
- protect your assets
- prepare your financial statements

Financial skills should include understanding of the balance sheet, the profit-and-loss statement, cash flow projection, break-even analysis, and source and application of funds. In many businesses, the husband and wife run the business; it is especially important that both of them understand financial management. Most small business owners are not accountants, but they must understand the tool of financial management if they are going to be able to measure the return on their investment. Although good records are essential to good financial planning, they alone are not enough because their full use requires interpretation and analysis. The owner/manager's financial decisions concerning return on invested funds, approaches to banks, securing greater supplier credit, raising additional equity capital and so forth, can be more successful if he takes the time to develop understanding and use of the balance sheet and profit-and-loss statement.

Balance Sheet:

The balance sheet, Figure I, shows the financial condition of a business at the end of business on a specific day. It is called a balance sheet because the total assets balance with, or are equal to, total liabilities plus owner's capital balance. Current assets are those that the owner does not anticipate holding for long. This category includes cash, finished goods in inventory, and accounts receivable. Fixed assets are long-term assets, including plant and equipment. A third possible category is the intangible asset of goodwill. Liabilities are debts owed by the business, including both accounts payable, which are usually short-term, and notes payable, which are usually long-term debts such as mortgage payments. The difference between the value of the assets and the value of the liabilities is the capital. This category includes funds invested by the owner plus accumulated profits, less withdrawals.

The Income Statement:

This statement, Figure II, is also known as a profit-and loss (P&L) statement. It shows how a business has performed over a certain period of time. An income statement specifies sales, costs of sales, gross profit, expenses and net income or loss from operations.

Figure I

Financial Forecast

Opening Balance Sheet - Date

ASSETS

Current Assets

Cash and bank accounts		$
Accounts receivable		$
Inventory		$
Other current assets		$ _____
TOTAL CURRENT ASSETS	(A)	$ _____

Fixed Assets

Property owned		$
Furniture and equipment		$
Business automobile		$
Leasehold improvements		$
Other fixed assets		$ _____
TOTAL FIXED ASSETS	(B)	$ _____
TOTAL ASSETS	(A+B = X)	$ _____

LIABILITIES

Current Liabilities (due within the next 12 months)

Bank loans		$
Other loans		$
Accounts payable		$
Other current liabilities		$ _____
TOTAL CURRENT LIABILITIES	(C)	$ _____

Long-term Liabilities

Mortgages		$
Long-term loans		$
Other long-term liabilities		$ _____
TOTAL LONG-TERM LIABILITIES	(D)	$ _____
TOTAL LIABILITIES	(C+D = Y)	$ _____
NET WORTH	(X-Y = Z)	$ _____
TOTAL NET WORTH AND LIABILITIES	(Y+Z)	$ _____

Figure II

Business Income and Expense Forecast for the Next 12 Months

One year estimate ending _____, 19 _____

Projected Number of Clients

For your services   _____

For your products   _____

TOTAL NUMBER OF CLIENTS   _____

Projected Income

Sessions $ _____

Product sales $ _____

Other $ _____

TOTAL INCOME $ _____

Projected Expenses

Start-up costs $ _____

Monthly expenses (x 12) $ _____

Annual expenses $ _____

TOTAL EXPENSES $ _____

TOTAL OPERATING PROFIT (OR LOSS) $ _____

CAPITAL REQUIRED FOR THE NEXT 12 MONTHS $ _____

Garden Center Business

Start-Up Costs Worksheet	
Item	**Estimated Expense**
Open checking account	$
Telephone installation	$
Equipment	$
First & last month's rent, security deposit, etc.	$
Supplies	$
Business cards, stationery, etc.	$
Advertising and promotion package	$
Decorating and remodeling	$
Furniture and fixtures	$
Legal and professional fees	$
Insurance	$
Utility deposits	$
Beginning inventory	$
Installation of fixtures and equipment	$
Licenses and permits	$
Other	$
TOTAL	$

Fixed Annual Expense Worksheet	
Item	**Estimated Expense**
Property insurance	$
Business auto insurance	$
Licenses and permits	$
Liability insurance	$
Disability insurance	$
Professional society membership	$
Fees (legal, accounting, etc.)	$
Taxes	$
Other	$
TOTAL	$

Monthly Business Expense Worksheet		
Expense	**Estimated Monthly Cost**	**X 12**
Rent	$	$
Utilities	$	$
Telephone	$	$
Bank fees	$	$
Supplies	$	$
Stationery and business cards	$	$
Networking club dues	$	$
Education (seminars, books professional journals, etc.)	$	$
Business car (Payments, gas, repairs, etc)	$	$
Advertising and promotion	$	$
Postage	$	$
Entertainment	$	$
Repair, cleaning and maintenance	$	$
Travel	$	$
Business loan payments	$	$
Salary/Draw	$	$
Staff salaries	$	$
Miscellaneous	$	$
Taxes	$	$
Professional fees	$	$
Decorations	$	$
Furniture and fixtures	$	$
Equipment	$	$
Inventory	$	$
Other	$	$
TOTAL MONTHLY	$	$
TOTAL YEARLY		$

Cash Flow Forecast						
	January Estimate	January Actual	February Estimate	February Actual	March Estimate	March Actual
Beginning cash						
Plus monthly income from: Fees						
Sales						
Loans						
Other						
TOTAL CASH AND INCOME						
Expenses:						
Rent						
Utilities						
Telephone						
Bank fees						
Supplies						
Stationery and business cards						
Insurance						
Dues						
Education						
Auto						
Advertising and promotion						
Postage						
Entertainment						

	January Estimate	January Actual	February Estimate	February Actual	March Extimate	March Actual
Repair and maintenance						
Travel						
Business loan payments						
Licenses and permits						
Salary/Draw						
Staff salaries						
Taxes						
Professional fees						
Decorations						
Furniture and fixtures						
Equipment						
Inventory						
Other Expenses						
TOTAL EXPENSES						
ENDING CASH (+/-)						

Cash Flow Forecast (Continued)

Notes _____

Chapter 6

Garden Center Business Planning

Introduction

Our increasingly service oriented economy offers a widening spectrum of opportunities for customized and personalized small business growth. Though untrained entrepreneurs have traditionally had a high rate of failure, small businesses can be profitable. Success in a small Garden Center business is not an accident. It requires both skills in a service or product area and acquisition of management and attitudinal competencies.

The purpose of this publication is to help you take stock of your interests, aptitudes and skills. Many people have good business ideas but not everyone has what it takes to succeed. If you are convinced that a profitable Garden Center business is attainable, this publication will provide step-by-step guidance in development of the basic written business plan.

Information Gathering

A helpful tool for use in determining if you are ready to take the risks of an Garden Center business operation is the SMA publication entitled *Going Into Business* (MP-12).

It will help you focus on the basic steps in information gathering and business planning.

Careful planning is required to research legal and tax issues, proper space utilization and to establish time management discipline. Inadequate or careless attention to development of a detailed business plan can be costly for you and your family in terms of lost time, wasted talent and disappearing dollars.

The Entrepreneurial Personality

A variety of experts have documented research that indicates that successful small business entrepreneurs have some common characteristics. How do you measure up? On this checklist, write a "Y" if you believe the statement describes you; a "N" if it doesn't; and a "U" if you can't decide:

_____ I have a strong desire to be my own boss.

_____ Win lose or draw, I want to be master of my own financial destiny.

_____ I have significant specialized business ability based on both my education and my experience.

_____ I have an ability to conceptualize the whole of a business; not just its individual parts, but how they relate to each other.

_____ I develop an inherent sense of what is "right" for a business and have the courage to pursue it.

_____ One or both of my parents were entrepreneurs; calculate risk-taking runs in the family.

_____ My life is characterized by a willingness and capacity to preserver.

_____ I possess a high level of energy, sustainable over long hours to make the business successful.

While not every successful Garden Center business owner starts with a "Y" answer to all of these questions, three or four "N"s and "U"s should be sufficient reason for you to stop and give a second thought to going it alone. Many proprietors who sense entrepreneurial deficiencies seek extra training a support their limitations with help from a skilled team of business advisors such as accountants, bankers and attorneys.

Selecting a Business

A logical first step for the undecided is to list potential areas of personal background, special training, education and job experience, and special interests that could be developed into a business. Review the following list of activities which have proven marketable for others. On a scale of "0" (no interest or strength) to "10" (maximum interest or strength) indicate the potential for you and a total score for each activity.

Time Management

For both the novice and the experienced business person planning a small Garden Center enterprise, an early concern requiring self-evaluation is time management.

It is very difficult for some people to make and keep work schedules even in a disciplined office setting. As your own boss the problem can be much greater. To determine how much time you can devote to your business, begin by drafting a weekly task timetable listing all current and potential responsibilities and the blocks of time required for each. When and how can business responsibilities be added without undue physical or mental stress on you or your family? Potential conflicts must be faced and resolved at the outset and as they occur, otherwise your business can become a nightmare. During the first year of operation, continue to chart, post and checkoff tasks on a daily, weekly and monthly basis.

Distractions and excuses for procrastination abound. It is important to keep both a planning and operating log. These tools will help avoid oversights and provide vital information when memory fails.

To improve the quality of work time, consider installation of a telephone line for the business and attaching an answering machine to take messages when you do not wish to be distracted or are away from your business. A business line has the added advantage of allowing you to have a business listing in the phone book and if you wish to buy it, an ad in the classified directory.

Is an Garden Center Business Site Allowable?

Now you will want to investigate potential legal and community problems associated with operating the business. You should gather, read and digest specialized information concerning federal, state, county and municipal laws and regulations concerning Garden Center business operations.

Check first! Get the facts in writing. Keep a topical file for future reference. Some facts and forms will be needed for your business plan. There may be limitations enforced that can make your planned business impossible or require expensive modifications to your property.

Items to be investigated, recorded and studied are:

TO DO   DONE

_____   _____   county or city zoning code restrictions
_____   _____   necessary permits and licenses for operation
_____   _____   state and local laws and codes regarding zoning
_____   _____   deed or lease restrictions such as covenants and restrictive conditions of purchase

_____	_____	parking and customer access; deliveries
_____	_____	sanitation, traffic and noise codes
_____	_____	signs and advertising
_____	_____	state and federal code requirements for space, ventilation, heat and light
_____	_____	limitations on the number and type of workers. If not, check with the local Chamber of Commerce office
_____	_____	reservations that neighbors may have about a business next to or near them

Here are some ways to collect your information. Call or visit the zoning office at county headquarters or city hall. In some localities the city or county Office of Economic Development has print materials available to pinpoint key "code" items affecting a business.

Even in rural areas, the era of unlimited free enterprise is over. Although the decision makers may be in the state capital or in a distant regional office of a federal agency, check before investing in inventory, equipment or marketing programs. If in doubt, call the state office of Industrial Development or the nearest SBA district office. In some states the county agent or home demonstration agent will have helpful information concerning rural or farm business development.

Is the Business Site Insurable?

In addition to community investigations, contact your insurance company or agent. It is almost certain that significant changes will be required in your coverage and limits when you start a business. When you have written a good description of your business, call your agent for help in insuring you properly against new hazards resulting from your business operations such as:

- Fire, theft and casualty damage to inventories and equipment
- business interruption coverage
- fidelity bonds for employees
- liability for customers, vendors and others visiting the business
- workmen's compensation
- group health and life insurance
- product liability coverage if you make or sell a product; workmanship liability for services
- business use of vehicle coverage

Overall Garden Center Site Evaluation

After you have gathered as much information as seems practical you may wish to evaluate several different locations. Here's a handy checklist. Using the "0" to "10" scale, grade these vital factors:

Factors to Consider

Factor	Grades 0-10
1. Customer convenience	_____
2. Availability of merchandise or raw materials	_____
3. Nearby competition	_____
4. Transportation availability and rates	_____
5. Quality and quantity of employees available	_____
6. Availability of parking facilities	_____

7. Adequacy of utilities (sewer, water, power, gas)   _____

8. Traffic flow   _____

9. Tax burden   _____

10. Quality of police and fire services   _____

11. Environmental factors   _____

12. Physical suitability for future expansion   _____

13. Provision for future expansion   _____

14. Vendor delivery access   _____

15. Personal convenience   _____

16. Cost of operation   _____

17. Other factors including how big you get without moving   _____

TOTALS   _____

Writing the Business Plan

Now that your research and plan development is nearing completion, it is time to move into action. If you are still in favor of going ahead, it is time to take several specific steps. The key one is to organize your dream scheme into a business plan.

What is it?

- As a business plan it is written by the Garden Center business owner with outside help as needed
- It is accurate and concise as a result of careful study
- It explains how the business will function in the marketplace
- It clearly depicts its operational characteristics
- It details how it will be financed
- It outlines how it will be managed
- It is the management and financial "blueprint" for start-up and profitable operation
- It serves as a prospectus for potential investors and lenders

Why create it?

- The process of putting the business plan together, including the thought that you put in before writing it, forces you to take an objective, critical, unemotional look at your entire business proposal
- The finished written plan is an operational tool which, when properly used, will help you manage your business and work toward its success
- The completed business plan is a means for communicating your ideas to others and provides the basis for financing your business

Who should write it?

- The Garden Center owner to the extend possible
- Seek assistance in weak areas, such as:
    — accounting
    — insurance
    — capital requirements
    — operational forecasting
    — tax and legal requirements

When should a business plan be used?

- To make crucial start-up decisions
- To reassure lenders or backers
- To measure operations progress
- To test planning assumptions
- As a basis for adjusting forecasts
- To anticipate ongoing capital and cash requirements
- As the benchmark for good operations management

Proposed Outline for Garden Center Business Plan

This outline is suggested for a small proprietorship or family business. Shape it to fit *your* unique needs. For more complex manufacturing or franchise operations see the Resource section for other options.

Part I - Business Organization

Cover page:

A.   Business name:

Street address:

Mailing address:

Telephone number:

Owner(s) name(s):

Inside pages:

B.   Business form:

(proprietorship, partnership, corporation)

If incorporated (state incorporation)

Include copies of key subsidiary documents in an appendix.

Remember even partnerships require written agreements of terms and conditions to avoid later conflicts and to establish legal entities and equities. Corporations require charters, articles of incorporation and bylaws.

Part II - Business Purpose and Function

In this section, write an accurate yet, concise description of the business. Describe the business you plan to start in narrative form.

What is the principal activity? Be specific. Give product or service description(s):

- retail sales?

- manufacturing?

- service?

- other?

How will it be started?

- a new start up

- the expansion of an existing business

- purchase of a going business

- a franchise operation

- actual or projected start up date

Why will it succeed? Promote your idea!

- how and why this business will be successful

- what is unique about your business

- what is its market "niche"

What is your experience in this business? If you have a current resume of your career, include it in an appendix and reference it here. Otherwise write a narrative here and include a resume in the finished product. If you lack specific experience, detail how you plan to gain it, such as training, apprenticeship or working with partners who have experience.

The Marketing Plan

The marketing plan is the core of your business rationale. To develop a consistent sales growth an Garden Center business person much become knowledgeable about the market. To demonstrate your understanding, this section of the Garden Center business plan should seek to concisely answer several basic questions:

Who is your market?

- Describe the profile of your typical customer

  Age?

  Male, female, both?

  How many in family?

  Annual family income?

  Location?

  Buying patterns?

  Reason to buy from you?

Other?

- Biographically describe your trading area (i.e., county, state, national)

- Economically describe your trading area: (single family, average earnings, number of children)

How large is the market?

- Total units or dollars?

- Growing _____ Steadily _____ Decreasing _____

- If growing, annual growth rate. _____

Who is your competition?

No small business operates in a vacuum. Get to know and respect the competition. Target your marketing plans. Identify direct competitors (both in terms of geography and product lines), and those who are similar or marginally comparative. Begin by listing names, addresses and products or service. Detail briefly but concisely the following information concerning each of your competitors:

- Who are the nearest ones?

- How are their businesses similar or competitive to yours?

- Do you have a unique "niche"? Describe it.

- How will your service or product be better or more saleable than your competitors?

- Are their businesses growing? Stable? Declining? Why?

- What can be learned from observing their operations or talking to their present or former clients?

- Will you have competitive advantages or disadvantages? Be honest!

What percent of the market will you penetrate?

1. estimate the market in total units or dollars

2. estimate your planned volume

3. amount your volume will add to total market

4. subtract 3 from 2

Item 4 represents the amount of your planned volume that must be taken away from the competition.

What pricing and sales terms are you planning?

The primary consideration in pricing a product or service is the value that it represents to the customer. If, on the previous checklist of features, your product is truly ahead of the field, you can command a premium price. On the other hand, if it is a "me too" product, you may have to "buy" a share of the market to get your foothold and then try to move price up later. This is always risky and difficult. One rule will always hold: ultimately, the market will set the price. If your selling price does not exceed your costs and expenses by the margin necessary to keep your business healthy, you will fail. Know your competitors pricing policies. Send a friend to comparison shop. Is there discounting? Special sales? Price leaders? Make some "blind" phone calls. Detail your pricing policy.

What is your sales plan?

Describe how you will sell, distribute or service what you sell. Be specific. Below are outlined some common practices:

Direct Sales - by telephone or in person. The tremendous growth of individual sales representatives who sell by party bookings, door to door, and through distribution of call back promotional campaigns suggests that careful research is required to be profitable.

Mail Order - Specialized markets for leisure time or unique products have grown as more two income families find less time to shop. Be aware of recent mail order legislation and regulation.

Franchising -

a. You may decide to either buy into someone else's franchise as a franchisee, or

b. Create your own franchise operation that sells rights to specific territories or product lines to others. Each will require further legal, financial and marketing research.

Management Plan
Who will do what?

Be sure to include four basic sets of information:

1. State a personal history of principals and related work, hobby or volunteer experience (include formal resumes in Appendix)

2. List and describe specific duties and responsibilities of each

3. List benefits and other forms of compensation for each

4. Identify other professional resources available to the business: Example: Accountant, lawyer, insurance broker, banker. Describe relationship of each to business: Example "Accountant available on part-time hourly basis, as needed, initial agreement calls for services not to exceed x hours per month at $xx.xx per hour."

To make this section graphically clear, start with a simple organizational chart that lists specific tasks and shows, *who* (type of person is more important than an individual name other than for principals) will do *what* indicate by arrows, work flow and lines of responsibility and/or communications. Consider the following examples:

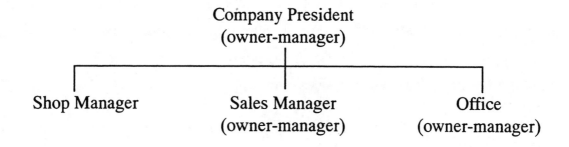

or like this?

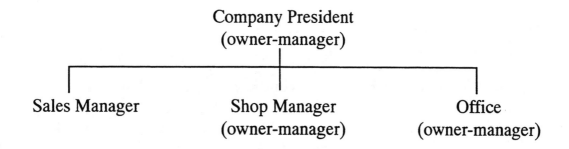

As the service business grows, its organization chart could look like this:

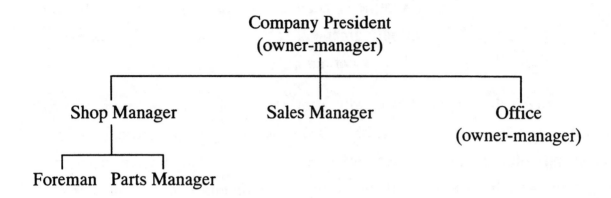

The Financial Plan

Clearly the most critical section of your business plan document is the financial plan. In formulating this part of the planning document, you will establish vital schedules that will guide the financial health of your business through the troubled waters of the first year and beyond.

Before going into the details of building the financial plan, it is important to realize that some basic knowledge of accounting is essential to the productive management of your business. If you are like most business owners, you probably have a deep and abiding interest in the product or services that you sell or intend to sell. You like to do what you do, and it is even more fulfilling that you are making money doing it. There is nothing wrong with that. Your conviction that what you are doing or making is worthwhile is vitally important to success. Nonetheless, the income of a coach who takes the greatest pride in producing a winning team will largely depend on someone keeping score of the wins and losses.

The business owner is no different. Your product or service may improve the condition of mankind for generations to come, but, unless you have access to an unlimited bankroll, you will fail if you don't make a profit. If you don't know

48

what's going on in your business, you are not in a very good position to assure its profitability.

Most Garden Center businesses will use the "cash" method of accounting with a system of record keeping that may be little more than a carefully annotated checkbook in which is recorded all receipts and all expenditures, backed up by a few forms of original entry (invoices, receipts, cash tickets). For a Sole Partnership, the business form assumed by this Management Aid, the very minimum of recorded information is that required to accurately complete the Federal Internal Revenue Service Form 1040, Schedule C. Other business types (partnerships, joint ventures, corporations) have similar requirements but use different tax forms.

If your business is, or will be, larger than just a small supplement to family income, you will need something more sophisticated. Stationery stores can provide you with several packaged small business account systems complete with simple journals and ledgers and detailed instructions in understandable language.

Should you feel that your accounting knowledge is so rudimentary that you will need professional assistance to establish your accounting system, the classified section of your telephone directory can lead you to a number of small business services that offer a complete range of accounting services. You can buy as much as you need, from a simple "pegboard" system all the way to computerized accounting, tax return service and monthly profitability consultation. Rates are reasonable for the services rendered and an investigative consultation will usually be free. Look under the heading, "Business Consultants," and make some calls.

Let's start by looking at the makeup of the financial plan for the business.

The Financial plan includes the following:

1. Financial Planning Assumptions - these are short statements of the conditions under which you plan to operate.

- Market health
- Date of start-up
- Sales build-up ($)
- Gross profit margin
- Equipment, furniture and fixtures required
- Payroll and other key expenses that will impact the financial plan

2. Operations Plan - Profit and Loss Projection - this is prepared for the first year's Budget. Appendix A-11.

3. Source of Funds Schedule - this shows the source(s) of your funds to capitalize the business and how they will be distributed among your fixed assets and working capital.

4. Pro Forma Balance Sheet - "Pro forma" refers to the fact that the balance sheet is before the fact, not actual. This form displays Assets, Liabilities and Equity of the business. This will indicate how much Investment will be required by the business and how much of it will be used as Working Capital in its operation.

5. Cash Flow Projection - this will forecast the flow of cash into and out of your business through the year. It helps you plan for staged purchasing, high volume months and slow periods.

Creating the Profit and Loss Projection.

Appendix A-11. Create a wide sheet of analysis paper with a three inch wide column at the extreme left and thirteen narrow columns across the page. Write at the top of the first page the planned name of your business. On the second line of the heading, write "Profit and Loss Projection." On the third line, write "First Year."

Then, note the headings on Appendix A-11 and copy them onto your 12-column sheet, copy the headings from the similar area on Exhibit A. Then follow the example set by Appendix A-11 and list all of the other components of your income, cost and expense structure. You may add or delete specific loans of expense to suit your business plan. Guard against consolidating too many types of expenses under one account lest you lose control of the components. At the same time, don't try to break down expenses so discretely that accounting becomes a nuisance instead of a management tool. Once again, Exhibit A provides ample detail for most businesses.

Now, in the small column just to the left of the first monthly column, you will want to note which of the items in the left-hand column are to be estimated on a monthly (M) or yearly (Y) basis. Items such as Sales, Cost of Sales and Variable expenses will be estimated monthly based on planned volume and seasonal or other estimated fluctuations. Fixed Expenses can usually be estimated on a yearly basis and divided by twelve to arrive at even monthly values. The "M" and "Y" designations will be used later to distinguish between variable and fixed expense.

Depreciation allowances for Fixed Assets such as production equipment, office furniture and machines, vehicles, etc. will be calculated from the Source of Funds Schedule.

Appendix A-11 describes line by line how the values on the Profit and Loss Projection are developed. Use this as your guide.

Source of Funds Schedule

To create this schedule, you will need to create a list of all the Assets that you intend to use in your business, how much investment each will require and the source of funds to capitalize them. A sample of such a list is shown below:

51

Asset	Cost	Source of Funds
Cash	$2,500	Personal savings
Accounts Receivable	3,000	From profits
Inventory	2,000	Vendor credit
Pickup truck	5,000	Currently owned
Packaging machine	10,000	Installment purchase
Office desk and chair	300	Currently owned
Calculator	75	Personal cash
Electric typewriter*	500	Personal savings

* A note about office equipment, test use or rent two or more brands that appear to meet your needs and select the one with which you feel most comfortable. Don't be afraid to ask others who have had to make this decision for advice. Compatibility of your system with those of potential typesetting services or printers should be of high considerations. If you are not quite sure, consider renting or leasing the equipment until you are. Service contracts on such complex electronic gear are usually a good insurance policy.

Before you leave your Source of Funds Schedule, indicate the number of months (years x 12) of useful life for depreciable fixed assets. (An example, the pickup truck, the packaging machine and the furniture and office equipment would be depreciable.) Generally, any individual item of equipment, furniture, fixtures, vehicles, etc., costing over $100 should be depreciated. For more information on allowances for depreciation, you can get free publications and assistance from your local Internal Revenue Service office. Divided the cost of each fixed asset item by the number or months over which it will be depreciated. You will need this data to enter as monthly depreciation on your Profit and Loss Projection. All of the data on the Source of Funds Schedule will be needed to create the Balance Sheet.

Creating the Pro Forma Balance Sheet

Appendix A-13. This is the Balance Sheet Form. There are a number of variations of this form and you may find it prudent to ask your banker for the form that the bank uses for small business. It will make it easier for them to evaluate the health of your business. Use this to get started and transfer the data to your preferred form later. Accompanying Appendix A-12 which describes line by line how to develop the Balance Sheet.

Even though you may plan to stage the purchase of some assets through the year, for the purpose of this pro forma Balance Sheet, assume that all assets will be provided at the start-up.

Cash Flow Projection

An important subsidiary schedule to your financial plan is a monthly Cash Flow Projection. Prudent business management practice is to keep no more cash in the business than is needed to operate it and to protect it from catastrophe. In most small businesses, the problem is rarely one of having too much cash. A Cash Flow Projection is made to advise management of the amount of cash that is going to be absorbed by the operation of the business and compares it against the amount that will be available.

SBA has created an excellent form for this purpose and it is shown as Appendix B. Your projection should be prepared on 13-column analysis paper to allow for a twelve-month projection. Appendix B represents a line by line description and explanation of the components of the Cash Flow Projection which provides a step-by-step method of preparation.

Resources

U.S. Small Business Administration
Office of Business Development

Business Development Publication
MP15

Garden Center
Business Associations for the Entrepreneur

Garden Centers of America (GCA)
1250 Eye St. NW, Ste. 500
Washington, DC 20005
Robert Dolibois, Exec. VP
PH: (202) 789-2900
Founded: 1972   Members: 1,025

Garden Council (GC)
500 N. Michigan Ave., Ste. 1400
Chicago, IL 60611
Gary Mariani, CEO
PH: (312) 661-1700   FX: (312) 661-0769
Founded: 1988   Members: 12,000

Notes _____

Chapter 7

Managing The Business

Delegating work, responsibility, and authority is difficult in a small business because it means letting others make decisions which involved spending the owner/manager's money. At a minimum, he should delegate enough authority to get the work done, to allow assistants to take initiative, and to keep the operation moving in his absence. Coaching those who carry responsibility and authority in self-improvement is essential and emphasis in allowing competent assistants to perform in their own style rather than insisting that things be done exactly as the owner/manager would personally do them is important. "Let others take care of the details" is the meaning of delegating work and responsibility. In theory, the same principles for getting work done through other people apply whether you have 25 employees and one top assistant or 150 to 200 employees and several keymen yet, putting the principles into practice is often difficult.

Delegation is perhaps the hardest job owner/managers have to learn. Some never do. They insist on handling many details and work themselves into early graves. Others pay lip service to the idea but actually run a one-man shop. They give their assistants many responsibilities but little or no authority. Authority is the fuel that makes the machine go when you delegate word and responsibility. If an owner/manager is to run a successful company, he must delegate authority properly. How much authority is proper depends on your situation. At a minimum, you should delegate enough authority: (1) to get the work done, (2) to allow keymen to take initiative, (3) to keep things going in your absence.

The person who fills a key management spot in the organization must either be a manager or be capable of becoming one. A manager's chief job is to plan, direct, and coordinate the work of others. He should possess the three "I's" — Initiative, Interest, and Imagination. The manager of a department must have enough self-drive to start and keep things moving. Personality traits must be considered. A keyman should be strong-willed enough to overcome opposition when necessary.

When you manage through others, it is essential that you keep control. You do it by holding a subordinate responsible for his actions and checking the results of those actions. In controlling your assistants, try to strike a balance. You should not get into a keyman's operations so closely that you are "in his hair" nor should you be so far removed that you lose control of things.

You need feedback to keep yourself informed. Reports provide a way to get the right kind of feedback at the right time. This can be daily, weekly, or monthly depending on how soon you need the information. Each department head can report his progress, or lack of it, in the unit of production that is appropriate for his activity; for example, items packed in the shipping room, sales per territory, hours of work per employee.

For the owner/manager, delegation does not end with good control. It involves coaching as well, because management ability is not required automatically. You have to teach it. Just as important, you have to keep your managers informed just as you would be if you were doing their jobs.

Part of your job is to see that they get the facts they need for making their decisions. You should be certain that you convey your thinking when you coach your assistants. Sometimes words can be inconsistent with thoughts. Ask questions to make sure that the listener understands your meaning. In other words, delegation can only be effective when you have good communications.

Sometimes an owner/manager finds himself involved in many operational details even though he does everything that is necessary for delegation of responsibility. In spite of defining authority, delegation, keeping control, and coaching, he is still burdened with detailed work. Usually, he had failed to do one vital thing. He has refused to stand back and let the wheels turn.

If the owner/manager is to make delegation work, he must allow his subordinates freedom to do things their way. He and the company are in trouble if he tries to measure his assistants by whether they do a particular task exactly as he would do it. They should be judged by their results — not their methods. No two persons react exactly the same in every situation. Be prepared to see some action taken differently from the way in which you would do it even though your policies are well defined. Of course, if an assistant strays too far from policy, you need to bring him back in line. You cannot afford second-guessing.

You should also keep in mind that when an owner/manager second-guesses his assistants, he risks destroying their self-confidence. If the assistant does not run his department to your satisfaction and if his shortcomings cannot be overcome, then replace him. But when results prove his effectiveness, it is good practice to avoid picking at each move he makes.

Notes

Chapter 8

Business Resource Information

Books

Steps To: Small Business Start-up,
   by Linda Pinson and Jerry Jinnett (Kaplan Publishing, 2006).

Blue's Clues for Success: The 8 Secrets Behind a Phenomenal Business,
   by Diane Tracy (Dearborn, 2001).

Entrepreneur Magazine's Start Your Own Business, 3rd. ed.,
   by Rieva Lesonsky (Entrepreneur Press, 2004).

MBA in a Day: What You Would Learn at the Top-Tier Business Schools,
   by Steven Stralser (New York: John Wiley & Sons, 2004).

Own Your Own Corporation: Why the Rich Own Their Own Companies and Everyone Else Works for them,
   by Garrett Sutton, Robert T. Kiyosaki, and Ann Blackman (Warner Books, 2001).

Portratis of Success: 9 Keys to Sustaining Value in Any Business,
   by James Olan Hutcheson (Dearborn, 2002).

Small Time Operator: How to Start Your Own Business, Keep Your Books, Pay Your Taxes, and Stay Out of Trouble, (Small Time Operator, 27th Edition)
   by Bernard B. Kamoroff, (Bell Springs Publishing, 2005).

Successful Business Planning in 30 Days: A Step-by-Step Guide for Writing a Business Plan and Starting Your Own Business,
   by Peter J. Patsula (Patsul Media, 2000).

Straight Talk About Starting and Growing Your Business,
   by Sanjyot P. Dunung (McGraw Hill, 2006).

Associations and Organizations

U.S. Department of Commerce
14th Street and Constitution Avenue NW
Room 5055
Washington, DC 20210
Phone: 202-482-5061
Web site: *rvwm.mbda.gov*

U.S. Department of Labor
200 Constitution Avenue NW
Washington, DC 20210
Web site: *www.dol.gov*

Federal Trade Commission
600 Pennsylvania Avenue NW
Washington, DC 20580
General information: 202-326-2222
Anti-trust and competition issues: 202-326-3300
Web site: *www.ftc.gov*

U.S. Small Business Administration (SBA)
403 3rd Street SW
Washington, DC 20416
Phone: 202-205-7701
Web site: *www.sba.gov*

SBA Regional Offices
• Region 1, Boston: 617-565-8415
• Region 2, New York: 212-264-1450
• Region 3, King of Prussia, PA: 215-962-3700
• Region 4, Atlanta: 404-347-995
• Region 5, Chicago: 310-353-5000
• Region 6, Ft. Worth, TX: 817-885-6581
• Region 7, Kansas City, MO: 816-374-6380
• Region 8, Denver: 303-844-0500
• Region 9, San Francisco: 415-744-2118
• Region 10, Seattle: 206-553-7310

Internal Revenue Service
Washington, DC 20224
Phone: 800429-1040
Web site: *www.irs.ustres.gov*

The IRS has an expansive Web site where you can find a great deal of tax help and a state-by-state guide for locating state tax information. There are also numerous tax publications (all numbered) including:

• Tax Guide for Small Business, Publication #334
• Self-Employment Tax, Publication #533
• Business Expenses, Publication #535

For tax forms go to *www.irs.ustres.gov/forms*

International Franchise Association
1350 New York Avenue NW
Suite 900
Washington, DC 20005-4709
Phone: 202-628-8000

American Association of Franchises and Dealers
P.O. Box 81887
San Diego, CA 92138-1887
Phone: 800-733-9858
Web site: *www.aafd.org*

Associations and Organizations

**National Association of Women
   Business Owners**
1411 K Street NW
Suite 1300
Washington, DC 20005
Phone: 202-347-8686
Fax: 202-347-4130
Information service line: 800-556-2926
Web site: *www.nawbo.org*

The National Association for the Self-Employed
1023 15 Street NW
Suite 1200
Washington, DC 20005-2600
Phone: 202-466-2100
Web site: *www.nase.com*
The NASE works to help the self-employed
make their businesses successful and provides
numerous benefits and services. It was formed
over twenty years ago by small business owners.

**Occupational Safety and Health Administra-
tion (OSHA)**
200 Constitution Avenue NW
Washington, DC 20210
Web site: *www.osha-slc.gov*

Institute For Occupational Safety and Health
Phone: 800-35-NIOSH or 513-533-8328
Web site: *www.cdc.gov/niosh*

Dun & Bradstreet
Austin, Texas 78731
Phone: 800-234-3867
Web site: *www.dnb.com*
For over 160 years, D&B has been providing
companies with information and assistance in
making key business decisions.

**American Entrepreneurs for
   Economic Growth**
1655 North Fort Myer Drive
Suite 850
Arlington, VA 22209
Phone: 703-524-3743
Web site: *www.aeeg.org*

**National Association of
   Home-Based Businesses**
10451 Mill Run Circle
Suite 400
Owings Mills, MD 21117
Phone: 410-363-3698
Web site: *www.usahomebusiness.com*

U.S. Census Bureau
Washington DC 20233
Phone: 301-457-4608
Web site: *www.census.gov*

U.S. Patent and Trademark Office
General Information Services Division
Crystal Plaza 3, Room 2CO2
Washington, DC 20231
Phone: 800-786-9199 or 703-308-4357
Web site: *www.uspto.gov*

U.S. Securities & Exchange Commission
450 Fifth Street NW
Washington, DC 20549
Office of Investor Education
   and Assistance: 202-942-7040
Web site: *www.sec.gov*

Associations and Organizations

**American Association of
Home Based Businesses**
Fax: 301-963-7042
P.O. Box 10023
Rockville, MD 20849
Website: *www.aahbb.org*

American Small Businesses Association
800-942-2722
8773 IL Route 75E
Rock City, IL 61070

Home Business Institute
561-865-0865
P.O. Box 480215
Delray Beach, FL 33448
Website: *www.hbiweb.com*

Marketing Research Association
860-257-4008
1344 Silas Deane Highway, Suite 306,
Rocky Hill, CT 06067
Website: *www.mra-net.org*

**National Association of the
Self-Employed (NASE)**
800-252-NASE (800-232-6273)
P.O. Box 612067
DFW Airport
Dallas, TX 75261-2067
Website: *www.nase.org*

Magazines

Entrepreneur Magazine, Business Start-Ups Magazine, and **Entrepreneur's Home Office**
Entrepreneur Media, Inc.
2392 Morse Avenue
Irvine, CA 92614
Phone: 714-261-2325
Web site: *www.entrepreneurmag.com*

Forbes
60 Fifth Avenue
New York, NY 10011
Phone: 212-620-2200
Web site: *www.forbes.com*

Inc. Magazine
38 Commercial Wharf
Boston, MA 02110
Phone: 617-248-8000 or 800-2340999
Web site: *www.inc.com*

My Business Magazine
Hammock Publishing, Inc.
3322 West End Avenue
Suite 700
Nashville, TN 37203
Phone: 615-385-9745

Consumer Goods Manufacturer
Edgell Communications
10 West Hanover Avenue
Suite 107
Randolph, NJ 07869

Minority Business Entrepreneur
3528 Torrance Boulevard
Suite 101
Torrance, CA 90503
Phone: 310-540-9398
Web site: *www.mbemag.com*

Workforce ACC Communications
245 Fischer Avenue
Suite B-2
Costa Mesa, CA 92626
Phone: 714-751-4106
Web site: *www.workforceonline.com*

Websites

www.allbusiness.com
A comprehensive site with resources for small and medium sized businesses.

www.bizweb.com
A guide to some 47,000 companies.

www.bplan.com
Numerous sample business plans for various industries.

www.bspage.com
The Business Start page includes a short course on starting a business, tips, and reviews of top business books.

www.business.gov
The U.S. Business Advisor is a one-stop shop for working with the many government agencies that impact upon business.

www.businessfinance. com
A major online source for finding potential investors.

www.businessnation.com
Business news, a library, discussions, opportunities, and resources.

www.businesstown.com
Information and articles from starting to selling your business.

www.catalogconsultancy.com
Information and guidance for catalog and direct mail businesses.

www.chamber-of-commerce.com
Links to local chamber of commerce Web sites, and e-mail addresses.

www.financenet.com
Sponsored by the US Chief Financial Officers Council, FinanceNet has a wealth of information and resources available specializing in public financial management.

www.globalbizdirectory.com
Massive director of retail, agricultural, mining, and numerous other business-related organizations and associations. Includes a state-by-state and international listing database.

www.gomez.com
Gomez offers business new and detailed report cards and consumer responses on e-commerce Web sites in various sectors.

www.homebusiness.com
Detailed information and business solutions for the home base business.

www.hoovers.com
Provides detailed business and company information, industry report links, professional help, business news, and more.

www.ideacafe.com
A good place for news, tips, expert advice ideas, and schmoozing with other small business owners.

www.inc.com
A wealth of articles and advice about starting and growing your business from the folks at Inc. Magazine.

www.marketingsource.com/associations
Find any association in any industry at this valuable resource site.

www.morebusiness.com
Articles, tips, sample business and marketing plans, legal forms contracts, a newsletter, and more offered for entrepreneurs.

www.nasbic.org
The National Association of Small Business Investment Companies promotes growth in the business sector through numerous programs.

Library Resources

Almanac of Business and Industrial Financial Ratios
(Prentice-Hall). Provides ratios and industry norms in actual dollar figures derived from IRS data. Each industry includes performance indicators such as total assets, cost of operations, wages, and profit margins.

American Wholesaler and Distributor Directory
(Gale Research). Provides listings of wholesalers and distributors sorted by product category and state.

Catalog of Catalogs
(Woodbine House). Contains descriptions and contact information for more than 14,000 catalogs, indexed by subject and company name.

Directory of Manufacturers' Sales Agencies
(Manufacturing Agents National Association). Lists manufacturers' sales agencies alphabetically and by state. Also has information on how to select a sales agent.

Encyclopedia of Associations
(Gale Research). Guise to national and international associations; contains contact information and descriptions; indexed by name, key word, and geographic area.

Financial Studies of the Small Business
(Financial Research Associates). Organized by industry; contains financial ratios and indicators for small and microbusinesses.

Lifestyle Market Analyst
(Standard Rate & Data Service). Reference book containing demographic and psychographic statistics for metropolitan statistical areas in the United States.

Small business Profiles
(Gale Research). Contains sources of information related to starting specific types of small businesses. Typical entries include start-up information, trade associations and publications, statistics, and supply sources.

Thomas Food Industry Register.
Directory of food manufacturers and suppliers to the food industry.

Thomas Register of Manufacturing.
Directory of most manufacturing firms; includes company profile and contact information.

The Small Business Administration

The U.S. Small Business Administration was established in 1953 to provide financial, technical, and management assistance to entrepreneurs. Statistics show that most small business failures are due to poor management. For this reason, the SBA places special emphasis on business management training that covers such topics as planning, finance, organization, and marketing. Often, training is held in cooperation with educational institutions, chambers of commerce, and trade associations. Prebusiness workshops are held on a regular basis for prospective business owners. Other training programs are conducted that focus on special needs such as rural development and international trade. One-on-one counseling is provided through the Service Corps of Retired Executives (SCORE) and Small Business Development Centers (SBDC). The SBA strives to match the needs of a specific business with the expertise available.

To access the SBA: Online http://www.sba.gov
                      SBA Answer Desk 800-827-5722

SCORE is a volunteer program that helps small business owners solve their operating problems through free one-on-one counseling and through a well-developed system of low-cost workshops and training sessions. To located a SCORE counseling center in your area or to consult online, access the following site: http://www.score.org
SBDCs are generally located or headquartered in academic institutions and provide individual counseling and practical training for prospective and current business owners. To locate a center near you, log on to http://www.sba.gov/sbdc.

A Concise Guide To Starting Your Own Business

Page A-2

Guide Overview

A concise overview of the complete guide to starting and operating a successful business.

The following topics are presented:

- Business Plan for Small Businesses.
- Getting Started
- Deciding Where To Start The Business
- Business Patronage Statistics
- Site Location
- Site Selection Criteria — Some General Questions.
- Choosing The Proper Method of Organization
- What Is A Corporation?
- Estimating Start-up Costs
- Preparing An Income Statement
- Preparing A Balance Sheet
- Marketing The Business
- Marketing Planning — An Outline for Marketing
- Advertising Media
- Management and Getting The Work Done
- Sample Organization Chart
- Summary of the Business Plan
- Guide Summary
- Reference Materials

Business Plan for Small Businesses

I. Type of Business

II. Location

III. Target Market

IV. Planning Process

V. Organizational Structure

VI. Staffing Procedures

VII. Control

VIII. Market Strategy

IX. Financial Planning

X. Budgeted Balance Sheet

XI. Budgeted Income Statement

XII. Budgeted Cash Flow Statement

XIII. Break-even Chart

————————————————————

Page A-4

Getting Started

Following is a list of what you need to accomplish to insure that your business endeavor will head in the right direction.

1. Define your educational background and work experience

2. Survey all basic types of businesses.

3. Define what type of business matches your experience and educational background.

4. Choose only the business that you would like to own and operate.

5. Define what products or services your business will be marketing.

6. Define who will be using your products/services.

7. Define why they will be purchasing your products/services.

8. List all competitors in your marketing area.

Deciding Where to Start the Business

Will your business fulfill a need in the area you plan to bring your business to? This section provides you with some important information you need to examine before taking your ideas any further:

1. Decide where you want to live.

2. Choose several areas that would match your priorities.

3. Use the list that follows as a guide to see if your location will match the estimated population needed to support your business. The numbers which follow the type of business indicate the typical number of inhabitants per year.

Business Patronage Statistics

Food Stores
Grocery Stores 1,534
Meat and Fish
(Sea Food) Markets . . . 17,876
Candy, Nut, and
Confectionery Stores . . 31,409
Retail Bakeries 12,563
Dairy Products Stores . . . 41,587

Eating and Drinking
Restaurant, Lunch Rooms . 1,583
Cafeterias 19,341
Refreshment Places 3,622
Drinking Places 2,414

General Merchandise
Variety Stores 10,373
General Merchandise 9,837

Apparel/Accessories Stores
Women's Ready-To-
Wear Stores 7,102
Women's Accessory and
Specialty Stores 25,824
Men's and Boy's Clothing
and Furnishings 11,832
Family Clothing 16,890
Shoe Stores 9,350

Furniture, Home Furnishings, and Equipment Stores
Furniture Stores 7,210
Floor Covering 29,543
Drapery, Curtains, and
Upholstery Stores 62,585
House, Appliances 12,485
Radios and TV's 20,346
Record Shops 112,144
Musical Instruments 46,332

Building Materials, Hardware, and Farm Equipment Dealers
Lumber and other Building
Materials Dealers 8,124
Paint, Glass, and Wallpaper
Stores 22,454
Hardware Stores 10,206
Farm Equipment Dealers . 14,793

Automotive Dealers
Motor Vehicle Dealers,
New and Used Cars 6,000
Motor Vehicle Dealers,
Used Cars only 17,160
Tire, battery, and
Accessory Dealers 8,800

Boat Dealers 61,500

Household Trailer Dealers . 44,746

Gasoline Service Stations . . . 1,395

Miscellaneous
Antique and Secondhand
Stores 17,170
Book and Stationery Stores 28,580
Drugstores 4,268
Florists 13,531
Fuel Oil Dealers 25,000
Garden Supply Stores . . . 65,000
Gift, Novelty Shops 26,000
Hobby, Toy, and Game
Shops 61,000
Jewelry Stores 13,400
Optical Goods Stores 62,800
Sporting Goods Store 27,000

From *Starting and Managing a Small Business of Your Own, 1973;*
Small Business Administration, Washington, DC

Page A-6

Site Location

1. Define your number of inhabitants per store.

2. Locate several sites/locations that will match your inhabitants per stores.

3. Define population and its growth potential.

4. Define local ordinances and zoning regulations that you will need in order to start your type of business.

5. Define your trading area and all competitors in your trading area.

6. Define parking need, for your kind of business.

7. Define special needs, etc., lighting, heating, ventilation.

8. Define rental cost of site/location.

9. Define why customers will come to your site/location.

10. Define the future of your site/location as to population growth.

11. Define your space needs and match with site/location selection.

12. Define the image of your business and make sure it matches your site/location.

Site Selection Criteria — Some General Questions

- Is the site centrally located to reach my market?

- What is the transportation availability and what are the rates?

- What provisions for future expansion can I make:

- What is the topography of the site (slope and foundation)?

- What is the housing availability for workers and managers?

- What environmental factors (schools, cultural, community atmosphere) might affect my business and my employees?

- What will the quality of this site be in 5 years, 10 years, 25 years?

- What is my estimate of this site in relation to my major competitor?

- What other media are available for advertising? How many radio and television stations are there?

- Is the Quantity and quality of available labor concentrated in a given area in the city or town? If so, is commuting a way of living in that city or town?

- Is the city centrally located to my suppliers?

- What are the labor conditions, including such things as relationships with the business community and average wages and salaries paid?

- Is the local business climate healthy, or are business failures especially high in the area?

- What about tax requirements? Is there a city business tax? Income tax? What is the property tax rate? Is there a personal property tax? Are there other special taxes?

- Is the available police and fire protection adequate?

- Is the city or town basically well planned and managed in terms of such items as electric power, sewage, and paved streets and sidewalks?

Page A-8

Choosing the Proper Method of Organization

Listed below are legal forms of business available to the small business entrepreneur:

Sole Proprietorship

Advantages
- Simple to start
- All profits to owner
- Owner in direct control
- Easy entry and exit
- Taxed as individual

Disadvantages
- Unlimited liability
- "Jack-of-all-trades"
- Capital requirement limited
- Limited life
- Employee turn-over

Partnership

Advantages
- Easy to originate
- Credit rating
- Talent combination
- Legal Contract

Disadvantages
- Unlimited liability
- Misunderstandings
- Partner withdrawal
- Regulations

Corporation

Advantages
- Limited liability
- Expansion potential
- Transfer of ownership
- Retain employees

Disadvantages
- Double taxation
- Charter restrictions
- Employee motivation
- Legal regulations

What Is A Corporation?

A corporation is an artificial being, invisible, intangible, and existing only in contemplation of the law," wrote Chief Justice John Marshall. In other words, the corporation exists as a separate entity apart from its owners, the shareholders. It makes contracts; it is liable; it pays taxes. It is a "legal person".

The corporation is the most complex of the three major forms of business ownership. The corporation stands as a separate legal entity in the eyes of the law. The life of the corporation is independent of the owners' lives. Because the owners, called shareholders, are legally separate from the corporation, they can sell their interests in the business without affecting the continuation of the business. When a corporation is founded, it accepts the regulations and restrictions placed on it by the state in which it is incorporated and any other state in which it chooses to do business. Generally, the corporation must report its financial operations to the state's attorney general on an annual basis.

Estimating Start-up Costs

Item	Amount
Fixtures and Equipment	$ _____
Building & Land (If Needed)	_____
Store and/or Office Supplies	_____
Remodeling and Decorating	_____
Deposits on Utilities	_____
Insurance	_____
Installation of Fixtures	_____
Legal Fees	_____
Professional Fees	_____
Telephone	_____
Rental	_____
Salaries and Wages	_____
Inventory if Retailing	_____
Licenses and Permits	_____
Advertising and Promotion	_____
TOTAL Estimated Start-up Cost	$ _____

Preparing An Income Statement

What is an Income Statement?

The income statement shows the income received and the expenses incurred over a period of time. Income received (sales) comes essentially from the sales of the merchandise or service which your business is formed to sell. Expenses incurred are the expired costs that have been incurred during the same period of time.

Plan A Budgeted Income Statement For One Year

1. Project Total Sales
2. Estimate Total Expenditures
3. Example Listed Below for Income Statement

Percents	1	2	3	4	5	6	7	8	9	10	11	12
Sales												
Cost of Sales												
Gross Profit												
Expenditure												
Rent Expense												
Supplies												
Wages/Salaries												
Utilities												
Insurance												
Depreciation												
Interest												
Miscellaneous												
Net Profit												

Preparing A Balance Sheet

What is a Balance Sheet?

The balance sheet shows the assets, liabilities and owner's net worth in a business as of a given date.

- Assets are the things owned by your business, including both physical things and claims against others.
- Liabilities are the amounts owned to others, the creditors of the firm.
- Net worth or owner's equity is the owner's claim to the assets after liabilities are accounted for.

A Budgeted Balance Sheet For One Year

- List all your business property at their cost to you: these are your assets.
- List all debts, or what your business owes on all your property; these are your liabilities.
- Take your total property balance (Assets), and subtract the total amount you owe (Liabilities).
- The balance is what you own in your business called (Owner's equity).
- Add Total Liabilities (2) & Total Owner's Equity (3).
- Listed on the next page is an example of a balance sheet.

NAME OF BUSINESS
BALANCE SHEET
DATE

ASSETS
Current Assets
  Cash
  Accounts Receivable   _____
Merchandise Inventories   _____
    TOTAL CURRENT ASSETS   _____

Fixed Assets
  Land
  Building   _____
  Equipment   _____
    TOTAL FIXED ASSETS   _____
      TOTAL ASSETS   1). _____

LIABILITIES
Current Liabilities
  Accounts Payable
  Note Payable   _____
  Payroll Taxes Payable   _____
    TOTAL CURRENT LIABILITIES   _____

Long-term Liabilities
  Mortgage Payable   _____
  Long-term Note   _____
    TOTAL LONG-TERM LIABILITIES   _____
      TOTAL LIABILITIES   2). _____

OWNER'S EQUITY
Proprietor's Capital   3). _____

    TOTAL LIABILITIES & OWNER'S EQUITY   (2 &3). _____

Marketing The Business

1. Define Your Market
   - Type of Customers
   - Age, Income, Occupation of your customers
   - Type of Trading Area

2. Promotion of Your Business
   - Advertising
   - Setting your Image

3. Customer Policy Plan
   - Develop a Customer Profile
   - Customer Services
   - Customer Needs

4. Pricing Your Products/Services
   - Know all your Costs
   - Know your Profit Margin
   - Know Competitor's Price
   - Know what Return you want on your Investment

5. Sales Promotion
   - Coupons
   - Contests
   - Displays
   - Demonstrations
   - Giveaways
   - Banners

6. Public Relations
   - Newspaper Article
   - Contact Trade Association
   - Radio Promotion
   - TV Promotion

7. Segmentation of your Market
   - Age
   - Occupation
   - Income
   - Location
   - Education
   - Hobbies

Marketing Planning

Outline for Marketing

I.   Product/Service Concept:
   a. Name of product or service
   b. Descriptive characteristics of product or service
   c. Unit sales
   d. Analysis of market trends

II. Number of Customers in your Market Area:
   a. Profile of customers
   b. Average customer expenditure
   c. Total market

III. Your Market Potential:
   a. Total market divided by competition
   b. Total market multiplied by percent who will buy your product

IV. Needs of Customers:
   a. Identification
   b. Pleasure
   c. Social approval
   d. Personal interest
   e. Price

V.   Direct Marketing Sources:
   a. Trade magazines
   b. Trade associations
   c. Small Business Administration (SBA)
   d. Government Publications
   e. Yellow pages
   f. Marketing directories

VI   Customer Profile:
   a. Geographical
   b. Gender
   c. Age range
   d. Income brackets
   e. Occupation
   f. Educational level

Page A-16

Advertising Media

Medium	Market Coverage	Type of Audience
Daily newspaper	Single community or entire metro area: zoned editions sometimes available	General
Weekly newspaper	Single Community	Residents
Telephone Directory	Geographical area or occupational field served by the directory	Active shoppers for goods or services
Direct mail audience	Controlled by the advertiser	Controlled
Radio audience	Definable market area	Selected
Television audience	Definable market area surrounding TV Stations	Various
Outdoor	Entire metro area	General auto drivers
Magazine	Entire metro area or magazine region	Selected audience

Management and Getting the Work Done

1. Define your objective for starting your business.

2. Define your goals: profit growth for first three years.

3. Develop an organization chart of your business.

4. Define your personal needs.
   - Hiring proper employees
   - Training employees
   - Motivation

5. Define all responsibility for each person in your business.

6. Define all authority.
   - Who will hire and fire?
   - Who will select and train all personnel?
   - Who will keep the important records as to inventory, purchasing, sales records, cash records, etc.?

7. Define all laws and regulations that will be requirements for operating your business.

8. Review all duties and tasks with all your employees.

9. Write a summary of all the important tasks that you want to finish in your first year in business.

Sample Organization Chart

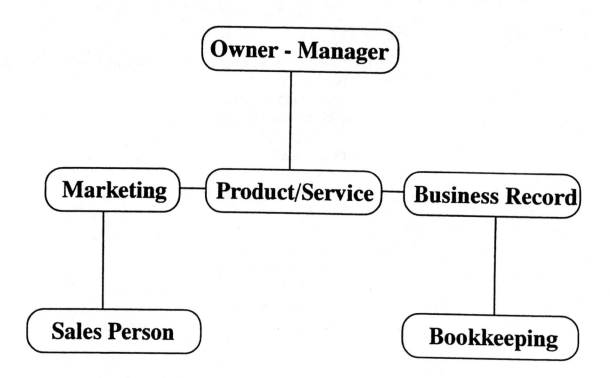

Summary of The Business Plan

Name of Business
BUSINESS PLAN
Date

1. Define your business
   - Name all principals
   - Address and phone number

2. Define your products or services

3. Define your market

4. Define your site or location

5. Advertising Plan
   - Budget
   - Media

6. Chart of Start-up cost

7. Worksheet of Income Statement
   - Revenue/Income
   - Expenses

8. Worksheet of Balance Sheet
   - Assets (Property)
   - Capital (Owner's Equity)
   - Liabilities (Debts)

9. Personnel Outline
   - Number of Employees
   - Staffing & Training

10. Management Organization
    - Organization Chart
    - Evaluation Policy
    - Job Profile

11. Special Statement
    - 3-Year Sales Schedule
    - Cash Flow
    - 3-Year Expense Schedule

Appendix A Summary

1. Contact your State Commerce Department for guidelines in starting your business.

2. Contact your City/County Clerk for guidelines in starting your business.

3. Contact all other Governmental Centers that will furnish you all the legal regulations and tax laws that will effect your business.
   - State Government
   - Internal Revenue Service
   - State Employment Security Commission
   - Department of Treasury
   - City Governmental Units

     a. Fire
     b. Police
     c. Zoning
     d. Building Permits
     e. Health
     f. Water & Sewage

4. Township Government
   - Local Legal Requirements
   - Local Taxes
   - Local Health Permits
   - Local Zoning Laws

Reference Materials

Management Aids Titles

Contact the

Small Business Administration
P.O. Box 15434
Fort Worth, TX 76119

for the following booklets:

- Number 2.025   Thinking About Going Into Business
- Number 2.010   Planning and Goal Setting For Business
- Number 1.016   Sound Cash Management
- Number 1.001   The A.B.C's. of Borrowing
- Number 1.008   Break-even Analysis
- Number 2.022   Business Plan For Service Firms
- Number 2.023   Business Plans for Retail Firms

Notes

Appendix B

HOUSEHOLD NEEDS

Many small business start-ups fail due to their inability to support their owners. Rarely do new businesses support their owners from the start. However, many individuals fail to recognize this fact. In addition, then, to a sound business plan, it is necessary for an owner to project the household cash needs month-by-month for the first three years of the business' operation. As a new business owner, you should be able to support yourself until your new business is able to support you in a manner to which you are accustomed.

MONTHLY HOUSEHOLD CASH NEEDS

Regular NON-BUSINESS Income
Spouse's salary _____
Investment income _____
Social security _____
Other income _____
Retirement benefits _____
Less taxes _____
Net monthly income _____

Regular Monthly Expenses

Housing
    Mortgage/Rent _____
    Utilities _____
    Homeowner's insurance _____
    Property taxes _____
    Home repairs _____

Living Expenses
    Groceries _____
    Telephone _____
    Tuition _____
    Transportation _____
    Meals _____
    Child care _____
    Medical expenses _____
    Clothing _____
    Personal _____

Insurance Premiums
    Life insurance _____
    Disability insurance _____
    Auto insurance _____
    Medical insurance _____

Debt Repayment
    Auto loans _____
    Consumer debt _____

Discretionary Expenses
    Entertainment _____
    Vacation _____
    Gifts _____ _____
    Retirement contributions _____
    Investment savings _____
    Charitable contributions _____
    Dues, magazines, etc. _____
    Professional fees _____
    Other _____

Total Monthly Expenses _____

Monthly Surplus/Deficit _____

Total Year Surplus/Deficit _____
    (Monthly x 12)

Available Assets to Cover Deficit
    Checking accounts _____
    Savings accounts _____
    Money market accounts _____
    Personal credit lines _____
    Marketable securities _____
    Lump-sum retirement/
      severance _____
    Other assets _____

Total Assets _____

NEEDED RESERVES
    Total Assets-Deficit _____

PERSONAL FINANCIAL STATEMENT

This is a picture of your personal financial condition to date. It is a very important part of any loan application and/or interview, especially when a loan for a projected new business is under consideration.

PERSONAL FINANCIAL STATEMENT

_____ _____ , 19 _____

Assets
Cash
Savings accounts
Stocks, bonds, other securities
Accounts/Notes receivable
Life insurance cash value
Rebates/Refunds
Autos/Other vehicles
Real estate
Vested pension plan/Retirement accounts
Other assets

TOTAL ASSETS $ _____

Liabilities

Accounts payable
Contracts payable
Notes payable
Taxes
Real estate loans
Other liabilities

TOTAL LIABILITIES $ _____

TOTAL ASSETS $ _____

LESS TOTAL LIABILITIES $ _____

NET WORTH $ _____

BALANCE SHEET

A balance sheet is a current financial statement. It is a dollars and cents description of your business (existing or projected) which lists all of its assets and liabilities.

BALANCE SHEET

_____ _____ , 19 _____

	YEAR 1	YEAR II
Current Assets		
Cash		
Accounts receivable		
Inventory		
Fixed Assets		
Real estate		
Fixtures and equipment		
Vehicles		
Other Assets		
License		
Goodwill		
TOTAL ASSETS	$_____	$_____
Current Liabilities		
Notes payable (due within 1 year)	$_____	$_____
Accounts payable		
Accrued expenses		
Taxes owed		
Long-Term Liabilities		
Notes payable (due after 1 year)		
Other		
TOTAL LIABILITIES	$_____	$_____
NETWORTH (ASSETS minus LIABILITIES)	$_____	$_____

TOTAL LIABILITIES plus NET WORTH should equal ASSETS

PROFIT AND LOSS STATEMENT

A profit and loss statement is a detailed earnings statement for the previous full year (if you are already in business). Existing businesses are also required to show a profit and loss statement for the current period to the date of the balance sheet.

PROJECTED PROFIT AND LOSS STATEMENT

	Month 1	Month 2	Month 3	Month 4	Month 5	Month 6	Month 7	Month 8	Month 9	Month 10	Month 11	Month 12
Total Net Sales												
Cost of Sales												
GROSS PROFIT												
Controllable Expenses												
Salaries												
Payroll taxes												
Security												
Advertising												
Automobile												
Dues and subscriptions												
Legal and accounting												
Office supplies												
Telephone												
Utilities												
Miscellaneous												
Total Controllable Expenses												
Fixed Expenses Depreciation												
Insurance												
Rent												
Taxes and licenses												
Loan payments												
Total Fixed Expenses												
TOTAL EXPENSES												
NET PROFIT (LOSS) (before taxes)												

CASH FLOW PROJECTIONS

A cash flow projection is a forcast of the cash (checks or money orders) a business anticipates receiving and disbursing during the course of a month. Well managed, the cash flow should be sufficient to meet the cash requirements for the following month.

CASH FLOW PROJECTIONS

	Start-up or prior to loan	Month 1	Month 2	Month 3	Month 4	Month 5	Month 6	Month 7	Month 8	Month 9	Month 10	Month 11	Month 12	TOTAL
Cash (beginning of month														
Cash on hand														
Cash in bank														
Cash in investments														
Total Cash														
Income (during month)														
Cash sales														
Credit sales payment														
Investment income														
Loans														
Other cash income														
Total Income														
TOTAL CASH AND INCOME														
Expenses (during month														
Inventory or new material														
Wages (including owner's)														
Taxes														
Equipment expense														
Overhead														
Selling expense														
Transportation														
Loan repayment														
Other cash expenses														
TOTAL EXPENSES														
CASH FLOW EXCESS (end of month)														
CASH FLOW CUMULATIVE (Monthly)														

Getting Down to Business...

How to Start & Manage a Garden Center Business

**An Instructional Guide
for Creating a Small Business
by Jerre G. Lewis, M.A.
and Leslie D. Renn, M.S.**

Notes _____

Planning a Garden Center

Unit One: Planning a Garden Center

Goal: To help you plan a garden center.

Objective 1: List three personal qualities a garden center owner might have.

Objective 2: Describe the services, customers, and competition of a garden center.

Objective 3: List one way to help a garden center "stand out" from its competition.

Objective 4: List two legal requirements for running a garden center.

Planning a Garden Center

There are many, many small businesses in America. Small businesses can have as few as one worker (the owner) or as many as four workers. A small business owner is "self-employed." Often a whole family works together in a small business.

Linda thought about four main things in planning her garden center. First, she decided that her personal qualities are right for the business. Second, she thought about her services, customers, and competition. Third, she decided to offer a special service so she can compete well. Finally, she learned about legal requirements for starting her business.

Services, Customers, and Competition

Services. Garden centers can offer many different services besides selling plants. They can sell plant supplies and garden supplies such as insecticides, garden tools, and even lawn mowers. Garden centers can also sell pots, plant hangers, and garden furniture.

Some garden centers are also nurseries that grow their own plants from seeds and cuttings. But even garden centers that buy their plants do some growing. Garden centers "nurse" some plants in pots or cans for two years or more before selling them.

Some garden centers offer landscaping services. Their workers help people plan what to plant around homes and businesses. Usually the worker makes a design showing where all the plants will go in the area.

A garden center can also sell cut flowers, flower arrangements, and houseplants. If the center sells houseplants, it usually has a small greenhouse for growing them.

Competition. Any place that sells plants can be competition for a garden center--even food and drug stores! Linda's main competition, however, will be the one other garden center in town. Linda feels that with her special business image and high-quality plants, she can attract enough customers. In fact, she feels her town is large enough to support two garden centers nicely. Linda decides not to focus on growing shrubs and trees because she does not think she can compete with her former boss--and she doesn't want to.

Special Services

To get customers, Linda needs to make her garden center "stand out." That way, customers will think of her when they need what she sells.

Linda has decided to make flowering plants her special product. She will have both outdoor plants and houseplants with colorful flowers. The name of her center will be "The Color Spot."

SUMMARY

It is important to plan ahead before starting your business. Now you know the important things to think about in planning a garden center: personal qualities you should have as the owner; your business' services, customers, and competition; and legal requirements.

Choosing a Location

Unit Two: Choosing a Location

Goal: To help you learn how to choose a location for a garden center.

Objective 1: List three things to think about in deciding where to locate a garden center.

Objective 2: Pick the best location for a garden center from three choices.

Choosing a Location

Choosing a location is important. You have to be sure that your services are needed in the area where you plan to open. Then you have to pick a spot where customers can find you easily. You need to learn a lot about the area to be sure your services fit. You can ask questions of the following kinds of people:

- people who might be your customers;
- people who have worked in garden centers;
- official garden center groups; and
- city or county agencies.

Once you are sure your services fit the area, you have to pick the spot for your business. There are five things to think about.

- The space has to be large enough for your needs.
- The building has to be where it will attract customers.
- It has to be built the way you need it. Sometimes you can remodel a place if it seems like a good spot.
- It has to be in good shape.
- The price has to be one you can pay.

Location

A garden center needs to be where people can see it and get to it easily. Many customers will learn about your shop just by passing it. So it must be located where many people can see it, or at least see its sign. Garden centers are usually on busy streets or in shopping centers. But nurseries that need lots of land usually locate in areas with fewer people.

Layout and Equipment

Neither of the spots Linda looked at had its own greenhouse. This meant she had to do some remodeling. The cost of remodeling is part of the cost of starting the business.

Sometimes you'll find a place that's just what you want. But many places may need some changes to fit your needs. a good location may be worth choosing even if it needs some changes. Just remember to include the cost of these changes in figuring out how much money you will need.

What it Costs

Your place has to be one that you can afford. To figure out what you can afford, you have to do a lot of thinking and planning about money. In the next section you will read about Linda's plans.

SUMMARY

Choosing a location is important. First, you have to be sure that your services are needed in the area you choose. Then you have to pick a good spot that will attract customers. Now you know some things to think about when picking a location.

Getting Money to Start

Unit Three: Getting Money to Start

Goal: To help you plan how to get money to start a garden center.

Objective 1: Write a business description for a garden center.

Objective 2: Fill out a form showing how much money you need to start a garden center.

Getting Money to Start

Starting a garden center takes money. There are many one-time expenses like remodeling and buying your first big order of plants.

Usually you need a loan from a bank or another lending agency. To get a loan, you need to give the loan officer three kinds of information in writing:

- personal information on yourself;
- a description of your business; and
- a statement of your starting expenses, money on hand, and loan needed, called a "statement of financial need."

Description of Your Business

Ms. Roundtree asked Linda to write a business description. A business description should tell the loan officer everything important about the business. A business description has five parts:

- kind of business and services provided;
- location;
- competition;
- customers; and
- plans for success.

Statement of Financial Need

Ms. Roundtree also asked Linda to fill out a statement of financial need. A statement of financial need has three main parts: starting expenses, money on hand, and loan needed. After Linda filled it out, it looked like this:

STATEMENT OF FINANCIAL NEED	
Starting Expenses	**Money on Hand**
Salaries . . . . $ 5,250	Cash on Hand $15,000
Building Expenses 4,500	Personal Loans 15,000
Repairs and Renovations . 20,000	
Equipment and Furniture . . . 1,000	Total $30,000
Inventory (plants and	
garden products) . 40,000	
Supplies (office & garden) 750	
Advertising 1,000	TOTAL STARTING EXPENSES $73,500
Other (insurance) 1,000	TOTAL MONEY ON HAND 30,000
TOTAL $73,500	TOTAL LOAN MONEY NEEDED $43,500

11

SUMMARY

You need to borrow money to start a business. You will probably have to borrow from a bank or another lending agency. Now you know that when you do ask for a loan, you will need to give a description of you business and a statement of financial need.

Being in Charge

Unit Four: Being in Charge

Goal: To help you learn how to plan work for the employees of a garden center.

Objective 1: Decide how to divide the work of the business among the workers.

Objective 2: Pick the best person to hire for a job in this business.

Objective 3: Describe one kind of training you might give your employees.

Being in Charge

Most small businesses hire extra workers at some time. To get good work done, you have to decide exactly what your worker should do. Then you have to find a good worker. A good worker knows how to do the job and also is reliable.

When several people work together, it is important that they get along. As the business owner, you must work at helping to keep your workers happy.

Dividing the Work

Linda decides to divide the work so that she does the selling and recordkeeping and Joe does the plant care. She could have chosen any of these ways to divide the work.

Hiring a Worker

After she finished the job descriptions, Linda put an ad in the newspaper. The ad said, "Wanted: person experienced with plants; will be responsible for daily plant care and buying plants and supplies; should have training and at least one year experience; part-time position, $6 per hour to start. Call 555-2875."

Using the newspaper is a good way to get workers. But not everyone who answers the ad will be a good worker. You should also ask each person about his or her training and experience. Then you can talk to the most experienced ones in person. Linda decided Tim didn't have enough experience. She only talked to Joe and Carol.

Linda went through five steps in choosing Joe to work for her:

- writing a job description;
- advertising the job to people who might want it;
- looking at training and experience of people who applied;
- talking to applicants about their work and about what the job will be like; and
- checking references from employers.

SUMMARY

Being a boss takes some thought. Now you know some ways to divide the work and some steps to follow in hiring a worker.

Buying and Keeping Track of Supplies

Unit Five: Buying and Keeping Track of Supplies

Goal: To help you learn to plan what supplies to order for a garden center and how to keep track of them.

Objective 1: Choose a supplier, decide how much you will buy, and plan a schedule for ordering supplies.

Objective 2: Compute the total amount of a purchase for your garden center.

Objective 3: Compute the amount of inventory on hand on a certain date.

Buying and Keeping Track of Supplies

In any business you will need supplies. In garden centers like Linda's, selling these supplies to customers is the business. In other businesses, you might sell services as well as supplies. For example, a landscaping service sells plants and designing and planting services. A service business usually needs fewer supplies But every business needs to buy and keep track of supplies. Supplies are also called "merchandise" and "inventory."

Choosing a Supplier

There are several places to find suppliers. Nurseries listed in the Yellow Pages of the phone book sometimes tell you that they sell "wholeslae." Tis means they do not usually sell to the public but instead sell at wholesale, or lower, prices to garden centers and other plant shops.

Another place to find suppliers is in trade magazines, where many suppliers put ads.

When and How Much to Order

Garden centers don't sell the same thing all year. In the spring they sell Easter lilies, annuals, seeds and vegetables. During the summer they sell fewer plants but sell many plant supplies. In the fall they sell bulbs, chrysanthemums, trees, shrubs, and mulches. And during the winter they sell poinsettias, Christmas wreathes, and maybe some barefoot trees and roses.

SUMMARY

It's important for any business to keep a careful track of supplies. You have to pick the best suppliers for your business. Then you have to use the purchase order and inventory card to keep enought supplies in stock. Finally, you have to know when and how much to order.

Setting Prices

Unit Six: Setting Prices

Goal: To help you learn how to set prices for plants and plant supplies.

Objective 1: Pick the best price for one item a garden center sells.

Setting Prices

Prices for garden center items can't be set wherever the owner would like. These are five things to think about it setting prices:

- <u>Cost of good sold</u>--In Linda's case, this is the cost of buying plants and plant supplies from her suppliers every month. It equals $4,000.
- <u>Operating expenses of the business</u>--These include the costs of the lease, Joe's salary, advertising, and insurance. They also include the costs of office supplies, payments to Mr. Sakamura, and other regular expenses. These add up to $3,000 a month.
- <u>Profit needed or wanted</u>--Linda needs at least $1,000 a month to live on, so she needs at least this much profit. Later, she will probably want more.
- <u>Demand for your products</u>--Customer's desires for different kinds of plants are not always the same. Lower demand means Linda must charge lower prices to get people to buy more.
- <u>Competition</u>--Linda has to charge about the same for her product as other garden centers charge. If she charges more, she will lose customers.

Operating Expenses of the Business

Operating expenses are the costs a business must pay just to keep its doors open, whether or not it gets any customers. For Linda's garden center, these expenses would include such things as:

- Joe's salary;
- her lease;
- insurance;
- advertising;
- office supplies;
- accountant and lawyer fees;
- utilities (water, electricity, telephone);
- supplies for caring for the plants in her shop (fertilizer, pesticide, etc.);
- maintenance of her shop and grounds; and
- interest on her loan.

Linda knows that her monthly income must cover these operating expenses as well as the cost of the goods sold.

Demand for Products

Linda knows that customer demand for certain plants can vary from time to time. One year maple trees may be popular; the next year birches or oaks may be more popular.

Competition

Linda has to be aware of the prices her competitors are charging for the same items. The best way for her to do this is to visit their shops now and then to compare prices. She can also check the newspapers to see the prices listed.

SUMMARY

You have to juggle lots of information to set prices. You have to know your business expenses: cost of goods sold, operating expenses, and profit needed or wanted. you also need to know what demand is like and what your competitors are charging. Setting prices for the hundreds of items in a garden center is a real challenge!

Advertising and Selling

Unit Seven: Advertising and Selling

Goal: To help you learn ways to advertise and sell the products in your garden center.

Objective 1: Pick one way to advertise this business.

Objective 2: Design a printed ad for this business.

Objective 3: List the six steps in selling.

Advertising and Selling

Advertising and selling are the major ways that businesses get customers. Selling is done person to person. Advertising includes all the nonpersonal ways of letting customers know about your business.

Other ways you can advertise include:
- signs on the shop;
- newspaper ads;
- direct mailings;
- radio announcements;
- billboards;
- fliers posted around town (such as those on bulletin boards);
- business cards; and
- give-away items like matches and pens

Advertising

When you plan an advertising campaign, it's important to ask yourself several things.
- Whom are you trying to reach?
- What do you want them to know?
- When should they know it?
- How can you reach them best?

What she wants people to know is what her store sells and where it is. So her ad tells these things.

When she wants people to know about her shop is a little before it opens. So she has to plan backwards to be sure of that. She talks to the newspaper almost a month ahead of time. Even before that, she had worked with an artist to get her design done. It's important to start early so your ad is printed when you want it to be.

Designing an Ad

A good ad is simple, truthful, and attractive. It tells the important things about your business. There are several things to work on in planning an ad.

Headline. The headline should attract attention to your ad. It should be short and give some important information about your business. Linda's headline is "Grand Opening," which gets the readers' attention!

Layout. The way the ad is laid out should be pleasing. It should not look "busy" or crowded with too many words. Readers must be able to see quickly what's important.

Selling

Some people think selling means "high pressure" selling. But trying to force a customer to buy is not good selling. In fact, it's the worst kind of selling, because the customer will probably never come back. If customers don't come back, you garden center will soon go ut of business.

Good selling means working to make the customer happy. Good salespeople have the following traits:

- They are pleasant, not pushy or phony.
- They are honest with customers.
- They are neat in appearance.
- They are proud of their products.
- They know a lot about their products and can give customers good information.

<u>**Selling substitutes**</u>. If a customer just doesn't like the product you have or if you're out of the product the customer wants, show a similar product. Explain why this product will meet the customer's needs. Be sure you're completely honest, or you may lose a customer!

(You can see that the last two steps don't happen in every sale. They happen only when the customer doesn't want the first item you offer.)

SUMMARY

You can have the best garden center in the world. But if people don't know about it, your business may fail. Advertising and selling are the ways you let people know about your products and get them to buy.

Keeping
Financial Records

Unit Eight: Keeping Financial Records

Goal: **To help you learn how to keep financial records for a garden center.**

    Objective 1: **Fill out a customer account form.**

    Objective 2: **Fill out a daily cash sheet for money received and paid out in one day.**

Keeping Financial Records

One of the most important things a small business owner has to do is keep good financial records. You have to know how much money is coming in and how much is going out. This is how you know if your business is making or losing money. Good records also help you report income and expense to the government to pay taxes. They can help you decide, too, if you should expand you business or cut it back.

Different businesses have different recordkeeping needs and methods. The needs of your garden center will be fairly simple. You will need a way to handle cash and credit sales and to keep track of the money coming into and going out of your business.

Daily Cash Sheet

At the end of each day Linda fills out a daily cash sheet. It has two purposes. It helps her keep track of the money that comes in --called revenues or income--and the money that goes out--expenses. You can see that it's an important form, because revenues and expenses are important parts of financial records. The form looks like this:

DAILY CASH SHEET				
Cash Receipts			**Cash Payments**	
Cash Sales	$	260	Salaries	$____
Credit Sales	$	46	Building Expenses	____
			Equipment and Furniture	____
			Inventory and Supplies	150
			Advertising	30
			Other	____
TOTAL CASH RECEIPTS	$	306	TOTAL CASH PAYMENTS	$ 180

Linda writes in two kinds of cash receipts. One is cash sales from the cash register. Today's total is $260.00. The other is money paid on past credit sales. Today's total is $30 from the Sims and $16 from Bob Tallchief, or a total of $46.

SUMMARY

Financial records help you keep track of your business income and expenses. Three of the financial record forms you will use are the sales slip, the customer account form, and the daily cash sheet.

Keeping Your Business Successful

Unit Nine: Keeping Your Business Successful

Goal: To help you learn how to keep a garden center successful.

Objective 1: Figure out the net profit, profit ratio, and expense ratio for this business.

Objective 2: State one way this business could increase its profits.

Objective 3: State one way this business could change its services to increase sales.

Keeping Your Business Successful

If a small business is successful for more than two years, it has a good chance of making it. Half of all small businesses go out of business before they've lasted two years. If a small business lasts for five years, chances of success are even higher. The Color Spot is still in business after two years, but Linda still has a ways to go before she earns a decent profit.

Profit and Loss Statement

A profit and loss statement shows income and expenses over a period of time, usually a year. Remember the daily cash sheets in the last unit? If you add the cash receipts and cash payments together for a whole year, you have most of the information needed for the profit and loss statement.

TWO-YEAR PROFIT/LOSS STATEMENT				
	YEAR 1		YEAR 2	
	$	%	$	%
Revenues				
Cash Sales	$ 30,000		$ 35,000	
Credit Sales	70,000		85,000	
TOTAL	$100,000	100%	$ 120,000	100%
Cost of Goods Sold	$ 50,000	50%	$ 60,000	50%
Gross Profit	$ 50,000		$ 60,000	
Expenses				
Salaries	$ 10,000		$ 17,000	
Rent & Utilities	20,000		20,500	
Supplies (ofc/grdn)	2,000		3,200	
Advertising	1,500		2,200	
Other	4,500		5,100	
TOTAL	$ 38,000	38%	$ 48,000	40%
Net Profit	$ 12,000	12%	$ 12,000	10%

SUMMARY

Keeping a small business successful isn't easy. The owner has to know how the market for services is changing. He or she also has to keep track of how the business is doing. Finally, the owner has to plan the best way to change services to keep the business going strong.

GARDEN CENTER SUMMARY

This module has been about owning a garden center. People with training in ornamental horticulture can start garden centers. They may also be able to run nurseries, landscaping services, and flower shops.

To start a small business, you need to do lots of planning. First you have to be sure that owning a small business is right for you. Then you have to decide what services to offer, how to compete, and what legal requirements to meet.

To pick a good location, you have to be sure that your kind of garden center is what people in the area need. Then you have to get the money to start. That means showing a banker that your idea is a good one.

Being in charge means dividing the work and hiring good workers. Then you must keep careful track of what you sell-- your inventory-- and figure out how much of each item to order.

Setting prices means figuring out the lowest price you can charge to meet your expenses and also the highest price you can charge and still be competitive. To do this, you need information on expenses and on your competitions's prices.

You also need to know about advertising and selling in order to get customers. Advertising lets customers know about your business. Selling means working to make the customers happy. These are both important ways to help you business succeed.

You should keep good financial records so you will know how the business is doing. then you can decide if you can expand your business or if you need to cut it back.

In order to own and operate a successful garden center, you need training in ornamental horticulture, work experience, and the special business management skills we have covered in this module. I you have not had a course in ornamental horticulture, you should take one before you decide to own a garden center. You can learn business management skills through business classes, experience, or by using the advice and example of an expert.

You may not make a lot of money by owning a garden center. However, you will have the personal satisfaction of being responsible for your business and making your own decisions. You can also decide when and how much you want to work. Think about how important these things are to you in considering whether you should start your own garden center.

Appendix D

INSURANCE CHECKLIST

TYPE OF INSURANCE	PURCHASE	DO NOT PURCHASE
PROPERTY INSURANCE:		
Fire	_____	_____
Windstorm	_____	_____
Hail	_____	_____
Smoke	_____	_____
Explosion	_____	_____
Vandalism	_____	_____
Water Damage	_____	_____
Glass	_____	_____
LIABILITY INSURANCE	_____	_____
WORKERS' COMPENSATION	_____	_____
BUSINESS INTERRUPTION	_____	_____
DISHONESTY:		
Fidelity	_____	_____
Robbery	_____	_____
Burglary	_____	_____
Comprehensive	_____	_____
PERSONAL:		
Health	_____	_____
Life	_____	_____
Key Personnel	_____	_____

More Information...

How to Start & Manage A Garden Center Business

An Instructional Guide for Creating A Small Business
by Jerre G. Lewis, M.A.
& Leslie D. Renn, M.S.

Notes

Planning a Garden Center

There are five main things you must do when you seriously start planning your shop: (1) decide whether running a flower and plant shop is right for you; (2) take a close look at your competition; (3) decide who your customers will be and the types of flowers and plants you will carry; (4) choose an image and a name that customers will notice and remember; and (5) learn about the laws for opening and running your business.

Products, Customers, and Competition

<u>Products</u>. Over the past ten years, sales of flowers and indoor plants have grown steadily. For some people, plants and flowers are ways of decorating rooms and offices. For other people, it is a fascinating hobby.

Plant stores are unlike flower shops and garden centers. The majority of plant stores sell only decorative house plants and related accessories. A flower shop, on the other hand, specializes in cut flowers and blooming plants. Much of a florist's business is done on the phone; therefore, a fast and efficient delivery service is essential. Garden centers and nurseries sell both indoor and outdoor plants as well as insecticides, fertilizers, garden furniture, and tools.

Small plant stores that helped make plants popular three or four years ago today face tough competition. Supermarkets, garden centers, department stores, and even drug stores now sell many kinds of plants. Florists have also begun to carry house plants. For this reason, many plant stores have started selling cut flowers. Store owners are having to expand their inventory in order to compete successfully.

The business of running a flower and plant store is tough. To succeed, you must follow customer tastes closely. As one plant store owner says, "Remember what your customers asked for that you didn't have, and buy it."

Customers. All types of people—young and old, rich and not-so- rich-buy plants and flowers these days. One reason is that, as cities grow, people feel they can't control their exterior environment. Therefore, they want to control their interior environment. The more concrete there is around them, the more people buy plants to soften the hardness.

In general, flower and plant stores sell to the full range of possible customers. To succeed, however, you should decide on the type of customer you particularly want to attract and then select your products, services, and store image to appeal to this group. For example, if your target customers are suburban women with expensive tastes, you might want to stock exotic plants, ornate planters, and extra decorative items for the home. If you want mainly to serve the "busy young working set" (many of whom live in apartments), you might specialize in house plants that are hearty and easy to care for and flowering plants that grow well in small pots on balconies.

Competition. Supermarkets, drugstores, department stores, and nurseries all compete with flower and plant stores. Supermarkets now sell many different kinds of plants and flowers; department stores often decorate their houseware sections with plants and flowers; even drug stores and gift stores will sell plants and flowers as sidelines.

These big businesses and stores give the small flower and plant store owner a lot of competition. However, there is still a place for the small plant store owner in this jungle. Offering a variety of flowers and plants together with personal service is the key to your success.

Helpful Personal Qualities

If you have a "green thumb" and like gardening, then owning a flower and plant store is a way of mixing business with pleasure. But being in the business world is very different from growing plants at home. In addition to gardening skills, you must know how to buy, sell, care for, and arrange flowers and plants. You should also have good "business sense."

It is helpful to have work experience in other plant stores. If you have studied ornamental horticulture and botany, you can use this information when you talk to your customers. This experience will help you convince customers of your knowledge and professionalism.

As a flower and plant store owner, spraying, watering, trimming, pruning, feeding, and repotting your plants will be daily concerns. The goal of all this work is customer satisfaction. The details of plant care must be spelled out to each customer. To run a successful flower and plant store, you must like people. You will be educating your customer about the plants they buy as well as selling the plants to them.

You will also have to learn many business basics. You will need to keep track of your inventory, income, and expenses. Unlike many businesses, running a plant store will let you combine your personal enjoyments of growing things with a healthy dose of business basics and a lot of hard work and enthusiasm. Your experiences in a florist shop and your experiences in business will help you in your new store.

How to Compete Well

Wise flower and plant store owners must look closely at their competition. Do these other stores sell quality merchandise? Do they sell many different types of plants and flowers? What are their prices? What services do they provide? What is their reputation? If they are successful, why? On the next page are some ways you can give your store an "edge" over your competition.

- Design the outside of your store in way a that will capture the attention of passers-by and make them want to come inside. A window display is the first contact a customer has with your flower and plant store.

- Use displays that include many different types of plants and flowers or focus on their decorative uses. Change your displays weekly to prevent plants from pooping out and to hold the interest of customers who pass by often.

- Offer your customers special services not offered by your competition. Your plants and flowers may be the same as everyone else's, but your services can make your store unique. Some flower and plant stores have been very successful offering services such as classes in plant care and flower arranging, plant clinics for "sick plants, plant-sitting services for people who are away from home, repotting services, delivery services, and so on.

Legal Requirements

Get in touch with your state licensing agency to learn about the licensee, taxes, and permits you will need to start a flower and plant store. Here is a fiat of things that may be required:

- a <u>sales permit;</u>

- a <u>business license</u>, available from the city hall or county courthouse;

- an <u>Employer' a Identification</u> (EI) number from the Internal Revenue Service; and

- a <u>floral association market badge</u>, which allows you to buy plants at the flower markets.

There are city and county zoning laws to be considered. These laws tell you what you can and cannot do to the outside of your store.

You will also need to buy insurance to protect your store. A basic plan may include fire insurance, liability insurance, crime coverage, automobile insurance (for company owned care), workers" compensation insurance, and business interruption insurance.

Summary

To start a flower and plant store requires a lot of planning. First, you have to decide that owning this kind of business is right for you. Then you have to decide who your customers will be, what types of plants and flowers to carry, how to compete, and what legal requirements to meet. There is a lot of competition in the flower and plant store business. To a great extent, the reputation of your store will depend on the quality of your merchandise, the services you offer, and the personal attention and care you give your customers.

Choosing A Location

Deciding where to locate your flower and plane store is a very important decision. The number of plants and flowers sold is directly related to the location of the store.

Choosing the Area for Your Store

Before you choose a location for your store, you will need to do some homework. If you choose a shop simply because it's close to home or is the first vacant store you find, you may be in for trouble.

Successful store owners know they need to consider a number of facts about the area where their stores are located. These include:

- the neighborhood's potential for growth;

- the ages, incomes, and interests of the residents;

- the competition in the area; and

- the type of neighborhood—urban, suburban, or commercial.

There are many places where you can get information on good areas to open flower and plant stores. Community banks, newspapers, census information, and chamber of commerce and utility company reports all provide information on the areas you may consider.

Questions to Ask When You Choose Your Site

Consider the next fiat of questions when you pick the <u>specific site </u>for your plant store.

- Who are your target customers?

- What business was in this location before you, and why did it close (or move)?

- How much competition will you have from similar stores in the area?

- Department stores and drug stores? Flower shops? Nurseries?

- Do a lot of people walk by this site? Is public parking available?

- In what condition is the street or store? Are repairs needed?

- How much apace will you need? Is there room to expand later on?

- What other kinds of stores are there in the neighborhood? Do they have many customers?

- How good is the heating, lighting, and ventilation of the building?

- What are the local zoning rule a and regulations?

City locations where there are many apartment buildings and offices are good places to open a plant or flower store. Since flower and plant stores depend on "drop in" customers for about 80% of their business, the store must be located on a busy street in town. The store should be easily seen by passers-by; a corner might be ideal.

Locating near other busy retail stores will help attract customers to your flower and plant store. If you are close to a busy shop or restaurant, you might be able to enjoy the "spill over" from their business. Many of the shoppers that buy flowers and plants in your store are customers of the art gallery.

The condition of the store is also important. You should check on the amount of light you will get. Will your plants get morning or afternoon sunshine? How much natural light comes in through the windows?

Flower and plant store owners have to spend a lot of time away from their stores in order to find and buy the right plants and flowers for their customers. The plant store owner must consider how closely the store is located to the flower and plant market suppliers and nurseries. How much time will be spent shipping the plants? Will they suffer if they have to travel long distances through all kinds of weather?

Store owners who are far away from their suppliers agree that distance limits the selection of plants. Certain plants do not "travel well." The distance will also add to operating expenses and will boost the price you must charge for your plants and flowers.

Renting and Leasing a Store

After you find a good location, you must arrange a lease with the building owner. These agreements are usually quite complex and may run over 40 pages. Lease or rental agreements should be reviewed by a lawyer and an insurance agent before they are signed.

Under a <u>flat rental system,</u> you will pay the building owner a fixed amount of rent each month. Rent may also be pan' under a <u>percentage of sales </u>agreement. In this case, you agree to pay a base amount and a percentage of the monthly sales. This type of system is often used in shopping centers.

Rent is a major expense. You must decide how much you can afford to pay or the basis of the amount of customers a location will attract. If you think a busy downtown site will bring you more customers, the extra money you'll spend on rent may be worth it. If, however, you think you'll have trouble paying rent in this "ideal' location, choose a slightly cheaper shop that's not quite as central—and do a better job of advertising.

Summary

A little logic and a lot of homework will go a long way when looking for the best location for your plant store. A highly visible downtown location with walk-in traffic will often be your best choice, even when the rent is high. The kinds of neighboring stores and the physical condition of the building are also important factors to consider when choosing a location.

Notes _____

Buying and Keeping Track of Supplies

Goal: To help you select your inventory and
develop an inventory control system.

Objective 1: Select the best flower and plant supplier,
decide how much you will buy,
and develop an ordering schedule.

Objective 2: Complete the total amount of
purchase order for your store.

Objective 3: Compute the amount of inventory
on hand on a certain date.

Notes

Buying and Keeping Track of Supplies

To a large extent, the reputation of your flower and plant store will depend on the quality of your merchandise. Your moat important concern is to buy and maintain top notch green plants and flowers. This is not at all like other stores, where you can rely on brand-name products. You must hand pick high-quality plants and flowers from reputable suppliers.

Some suppliers may specialize in plants or cut flowers, while others may deal only with supplies. Many suppliers handle a full line of flowers, greenery, and supplies. Your choice of suppliers will depend on what merchandise and services you plan to emphasize and the services each supplier offers. In this unit you will learn how to choose your merchandise and suppliers, and how to manage and control your inventory.

Inventory Selection

Here are some basic points to keep in mind when buying plants and flowers.

- <u>Buy what you know will sell</u>. Standard ornamentals—philodendrons, ferns, Jade trees, ivies, and coleuses—are very popular and form a good basic plant inventory. Carnations, roses, gladioli, and chrysanthemums are among the most popular flowers. However, each flower and plant store sells to different customers. What will sell in one store may not sell in another. You should buy what your customers want.

- <u>Keep a small selection of "specimen" plants and flowers</u>. Specimen items are usually the larger, more expensive plants and flowers. They add color and character to a store. You may not sell many of these specimens, but they can add character and variety to your inventory.

- <u>Include some rare and exotic plants and flowers</u>. Store owners know that customers tire quickly of the "some old stuff." To fight this boredom and to add a little variety to your store, you may wish to add plants like burro's tails or staghorn ferns, or some of the more unusual orchids. If you include a selection of herbs in your inventory, you will really be adding a "little bit of spice" to your store.

- <u>Buy what you like, but keep your customers in mind</u>. Store owners often buy the plants and flowers they like. But when in doubt, the customers' tastes must come first.

- <u>Be flexible</u>. You cannot always go to your suppliers with a fiat of what you want to carry in your store. Growers and suppliers may not have those plants and flowers in stock. You will have keep an open mind about your store's inventory. This is actually an advantage—when you go to your grower, you might just happen to see a plant you wouldn't have noticed otherwise.

- <u>Don't over-buy</u>. Once in a while, a grower or supplier might have a special on certain plants or flowers. You might be tempted to buy many of these plants. Avoid loading up on too many plants or flowers. What you can't sell may die, or you may simply end up boring your customers. After all, what can you do with 200 cactuses?.

Choosing Suppliers

Plant store owners get their supplies and inventory from three different sources.

- Plant growers and wholesalers supply plants and flowers.

- Wholesale flower markets offer a wide selection of cut flowers and plants.

- Garden supply distributors sell "hard goods" such as pots foods, and potting soil.

Before you open your store, you will have to find reliable flower and plant suppliers. Most flower and plant store owners will have accounts with eight or more plant growers. However, if there is a wholesale flower market in your area, you may be able to buy all your cut flowers and plants in one place.

To buy quality merchandise, you will often have to spend mornings away from the store. It is wise to try to find growers within easy traveling distance to your store. In this way, you can visit two or three in the same morning.

The wholesale flower market distributes the flowers and greenery that come from the growers. A wholesale market may be able to supply all the inventory needs of your store. This is simpler than trying to buy your inventory from many different growers. However, you may lose out on the special benefits, services, and individualized attention that come from building personal relationships with growers and suppliers. Also, the prices may be somewhat higher for the same merchandise.

You should keep the number of suppliers small. Here are some consideration in choosing them.

- Some growers will let store owners call in their orders before picking them up. This will cut down on the time you have to spend away from the store.

- Some growers will deliver to your store, depending on the size of the order.

- Suppliers will favor their more loyal customers, especially if they know you personally. You may be given preferential treatment in flower and plant selection and delivery service. The supplier will be more helpful if, for any reason, the customer is not satisfied with an order. You will hear tips on plants in stock "from the horse's mouth." You will get better attention for special orders for your customers.

Purchase Orders

You now have enough information to fill out a purchase order.

PURCHASE ORDER

TO: _____   DATE: _____

_____   PURCHASE ORDER NUMBER: _____

_____   REQUIRED DELIVERY DATE: _____

SHIP TO: _____   SHIP VIA: _____

_____

_____

Quantity	Unit	Description	Unit Cost	Total Cost

TOTAL _____

Signature _____

The form you use may be slightly different. The important thing is that you have accurate records of what you purchase and the money you spend.

Inventory Control

It's great to get lost in your own green jungle. To many flower and plant store owners, keeping track of inventory means a return to the ordinary world of numbers.

There are several reasons to have some kind of inventory control system:

- to keep track of plants and flowers that go into and out of a store;

- to help you plan for future orders;

- to give you an idea of the dollar value of your inventory; and

- to let you know which plants and flowers sell well and which ones are "losers."

Keep your inventory control system simple. <u>Personal observation</u> is one way of keeping track of stock. By arranging your displays in a certain order—four inch pots on one shelf, six inch pots on another—you can tell by looking what has been sold and what needs to be reordered.

You can also take <u>physical inventory counts</u> to get a precise number of items still on the shelf. This should be done on a regular basis, perhaps weekly.

Store owners must keep accurate records of their sales. 'This is a sample inventory card you can use to record your purchases and sales:

INVENTORY CARD

Item _____

Supplier _____

Reorder Point _____ Reorder Amount _____

AMOUNT RECEIVED		AMOUNT SOLD		AMOUNT REMAINING	
Date	Amount	Date	Amount	Date	Amount

Summary

It is important to find reliable suppliers of your plants and flowers—whether you buy from individual growers or at a flower market. It is also very important to keep accurate and up-to-date records of your purchases and sales.

Setting Prices

There are four main things to consider in setting the prices of the plants and flowers in your store:

- the wholesale coat of your merchandise;

- the labor and operating costs of your store;

- the amount of profit you want to make on your sales; and

- your competition's prices.

In this unit you will learn about how to set prices, including marking up and marking down prices. You will also learn about stock turnover, an important sign of your store's success.

Pricing

A basic step in making a profit in your store is selling plants and flowers for more than they cost you. But how to decide on prices that are competitive, will bring customers in, and are profitable for you is a real challenge for many flower and plant store owners.

The wholesale prices of plants and flowers may go up and down daily, without any warning. A plant that coats you $10 on Friday nay coat $15 on Monday. And there are often flower and plant shortages' When this happens, you have to choose between going without and trying to find the plants and flowers at other suppliers or growers who may be less reliable.

As a result of these problems, some flower and plant store owners change their prices often. But this involves a lot of work. Other plant store owners rely on standard markups to cover their expenses. The difference between the wholesale cost of the merchandise and the retail price is called <u>markup</u>. You should chose to use a standard markup to figure the prices for their plants and flowers.

The prices on your plants and flowers have to stay within a competitive range or your customers will start buying at other stores. But prices must be set high enough so that your operating and selling expenses are covered. The best policy for your store may become clear to you only after a very careful look at your business practices and your competition.

The most common pricing strategy is called gross profit pricing Gross profit is the amount you add to the wholesale coat of your merchandise. (Here, gross profit equals markup.) For example, if the coat of a philodendron is $8.00 and you sell it for $20.00, your "gross profit is $12.00, or 60X of your selling price.

You can use the following formula to calculate your gross per percentage:

$$\frac{\text{Selling Price} - \text{Wholesale Cost}}{\text{Selling Price}} = \text{Gross Profit Percentage}$$

$$\frac{\$20.00 - \$8.00}{\$20.00} = 60\%$$

Remember, though, that your net profit will be much less than this figure. The store's operating expenses must come out of the gross profit. These expenses may include:

- transportation costs;

- rent for the store;

- salaries of salespeople;

- advertising and promotion costs; and

- utilities, insurance fees, and taxes.

Markups on plants and flowers will vary from one store to another. Most flower and plant store owners mark up their plants and flowers between 100% and 300X. Hard goods are usually marked up around 100%.

Markdown Sales

If your plants and flowers are not selling, you may consider marking them down for quick sale. Remember, flowers wilt with time, and plants age and die. It may take more effort on your part to try to bring a plant back to life than it is worth. And unsold flowers will eventually have to be thrown out.

You may also consider marking down prices on plants that are healthy but slow-moving. If you hold on to slow-moving stock, you freeze the money you need to buy newer, more appealing kinds of plants and flowers.

Some plant stores have special corners to handle their markdowns and sale items. Other stores may have two to four big sales each year. There are many kinds of sales. Certain holidays are particularly good selling times for plants and flowers.

There is a large demand for plants at Christmas time. Valentine's Day is also a favorite day to send flowers to loved ones. But the day when the largest number of plants and flowers are sold is Mother's Day!

If a plant has been around for a long time, you may even consider selling it <u>below coat</u>. These plants and flowers may be used to attract customers to your store. Although you will not be making money on the sale, you may be making some surprised customer very happy. You will also be clearing the store for newer and fresher plants and flowers.

Stock Turnover

<u>Stock turnover</u> is the number of times a store's inventory is sold and has to be replaced in a given time period—usually a year.

A healthy flow of goods in and out of your store is important for its success. Stock turnover is one sign of a successful flower and plant store operation.

Most stores try to sell their merchandise as fast as they can. This way they have ready cash to buy new merchandise and to improve their inventory. Here is how to figure your turnover rate:

$$\frac{\text{Cost of Goods Sold in One Year}}{\text{Average Cost of Inventory Carried}} = \text{Turnover Rate}$$

To figure your <u>average inventory</u>, add the wholesale costs of all your inventory on hand on January 1. Include all your plants, flowers, and hard goods (plant foods, fertilizers, accessories, and so on). Then count and add the wholesale costs of your end-of- month inventories for the next 12 months. Add these two figures together and divide by 13.

Average turnover rates can be used to see how well your business is doing. In general, flower and plant shop owners come up with turnover rates of between 9 and 12 times a year.

If your turnover rate is higher than this, it may mean that you need to buy in larger quantities. On the other hand, a low turnover rate may mean slow sales or a poor choice of inventory. An average turnover rate will tell you that you have bought well. You have a well planned stock that meets the demands of your customers.

Summary

There are four main things to consider when setting prices for your plans a and flowers: wholesale costs; operating coats; competition; and profit. A well-planned, competitive pricing policy should help your store show a good profit. In addition, a healthy stock turnover is a good measure of the success of your store.

Notes _____

SUMMARY

Starting a flower and plant store requires a lot of planning. First, you have to decide that owning this kind of business is right for you. Then you have to decide who your customers will be, what types of plants and flowers to carry, how to compete, and what legal requirements to meet. There is a lot of competition in the flower and plant business. To a great extent, the reputation of your store will depend on the quality of your merchandise, the services you offer, and the personal attention and care you give your customers.

When choosing a location for your store, a highly visible down town spot with walking traffic will often be your best choice, even when the rent is high. When you apply for a loan to start your flower and plant store, you will need to provide a business plan and a statement of financial need. The bank will need to know your specific financial plane in order to lend you money.

Dividing work responsibilities and managing your staff well can help your store succeed. Screening and interviewing job applicants, providing training, establishing communication channels, offering good salaries, and defining your store policies are basic to success.

It is important to find reliable suppliers of your plants and flowers. It is also very important to keep accurate and up-to-date records of your purchases and sales, using purchase orders and inventory cards.

There are four main things to consider when setting prices for your plants and flowers: wholesale costs; operating expenses; competition; and desired profit. In addition, being aware of your stock turnover is important to the success of your business.

Advertising and selling are the ways you let people know about your business and get them to buy. Your advertising campaign should be well planned, distinctive, and consistent with your store's image. There are many ways to advertise, including direct mailings, the Yellow Pages, newspapers, and radio. However, personal references from satisfied customers are your strongest advertising method; and good selling techniques produce satisfied customers.

Keeping good financial records is another necessary part of owning and operating a flower and plant store. Cash and credit sales should be recorded on sales slips and customer billing forms. Daily cash sheets will help you keep track of daily revenues and expenses. By keeping these records, you can figure out your profits and compare them year-to- year by recording your income and expenses on profit/loss statements. If you want to increase profits, you must increase sales, raise prices, or reduce expenses.

To own and operate a successful flower and plant store, you need training in ornamental horticulture, work experience, and the special business management skills we have covered in this module. You can learn business management skills through business classes, experience, or by using the advice and example of an expert.

You may not make a lot of money owning a flower and plant store. However, you will have the personal satisfaction of being responsible for your business and making your own decisions. Think about how important these things are to you in considering whether you should start your own flower and plant store.

Special Appendix

Web Site Marketing

Business Web Site
an
Effective Marketing Tool

More than 100 million people use the Internet each day. A website offers help in marketing your small business. Your web site can help level the playing field for small businesses who compete with big businesses. It can enable small business to expand their business nationally or internationally.

What makes a good web site?

A good web site shows by doing; it proves rather than states. Instead of making claims, it provides evidence.

Evidence can take several forms:

- Case Studies showing how your efforts solved a previous client's problems.

- Testimonials from satisfied clients.

- Reprints of articles you've written or reviews of your work.

Education, however, remains the best way to establish credibility. To the extent prospects leave your web site better informed about your product or service, the easier it is to gain their respect (and their purchase order).

Three steps to creating your own business web site.

Today's tools make web publishing accessible to small businesses without programming experience. For example, Microsoft® Publisher 97 includes PageWizard design assistants, web deign elements and design checkers to help your build a workable web site.

Step one:

Choose a structure and a look. Your site should be structured and designed to best tell your story. But where do you start? Using the Page Wizard, you can choose from pre-designed options that can later be customized so that establishing a structure and "look" is easy.

Step two:

Tell your story. Next, simply select the sample headlines and text provided and replace them with words that describe what you have to offer.

Step three:

Check your work and post your site. The design in Publisher 97 goes through your web site element by element, identifying potential problems. Then, the web publishing wizard guides you through the process of posting your web site on the local Internet service provider or on-line service of your choice.

Remember, with millions of web sites, you may have to market your web site as well as your small business to get traffic for your business. The web site can be an inexpensive way of effectively building your small business.

10 tips for Web Site Online Marketing

1. Put up a simple web page.
2. Use a name that will attract people
3. Give away advice and information
4. Have lots of e-mail correspondence
5. Provide customized pages for users.
6. Visit user groups
7. Get on mailing lists
8. Arrange links with related sites
9. Make sure you're in every possible directory
10. Do not "SPAM"

INDEX

Step-by-Step Guides
To Start, Manage & Market
Your Own Business

4th Printing!

New!

3rd Printing!

How To Start & Manage Your Own Business

For anyone who is looking to start-up a new business, this *step-by-step guide* includes planning, managing, marketing and promotion.

$21.95

Soft Cover • 104 Pages
5 1/2" x 8 1/2" 0-9628759-0-2 ©1992

How to Start & Manage a Home Based Business

This book provides the knowledge and tools necessary to successfully plan, design, and start up a new business in a practical way. With a step-by-step guide for planning, managing, marketing and promotion of a small business, in an easy-to-read and easy-to-understand format. The guidelines presented will help you pursue dreams of independence and financial success.

$21.95

Soft Cover • 135 Pages
5 1/2" x 8 1/2" 1-887005-11-0 © 1996

How To Start A Participative Management Program

A concise guide for small to midsize companies that is easy to read and follow *Step-by-step planning, managing and marketing of a small business* • How to empower and involve employees • Contains tools for measuring employees work environment.

$21.95

Soft Cover • 93 Pages •
5 1/2" x 8 1/2", 0-9628759 ©1992

ABOUT THE AUTHORS

Jerre G. Lewis and Leslie D. Renn are both experienced professionals concerning small business management and entrepreneurship. For more than twenty years Mr. Lewis has been involved with business education at college level and the development of a series of small business seminars. He is a Certified Education Specialist for the U.S. Small Business Administration Volunteer Counseling Program. Mr. Renn is a business owner, entrepreneur, a small business consultant, and like Mr. Lewis, is involved with college level management instruction & business seminars. He also has extensive experience in large industry administration. Mr. Lewis and Mr. Renn received bachelors and masters degrees from Michigan universities, and both work and live in northern Michigan.

TO ORDER BUSINESS PLANS

Please Remit To:

LEWIS AND RENN ASSOCIATES
10315 HARMONY DRIVE
INTERLOCHEN, MICHIGAN 49643

Business Book # _____ Title _____
Business Book # _____ Title _____

Name _____
Address _____
City _____
State _____ Zip _____

Business Book _____
U.S. Shipping & Postage $ 3.00
Total _____

Business Books

Telephone 1-231-275-7287 • Fax 1-231-275-7242 • lewisjv@centurytel.net
Telephone 1-480-807-9530 • Fax 1-480-830-1187 • lrenn@cox.net

How to Start and Manage:

ISBN 978-1-57916-152-1   An Apparel Store Business
ISBN 978-1-57916-153-8   A Word Processing Service Business
ISBN 978-1-57916-154-5   A Garden Center Business
ISBN 978-1-57916-155-2   A Hair Styling Shop Business
ISBN 978-1-57916-156-9   A Bicycle Shop Business
ISBN 978-1-57916-157-6   A Travel Agency Business
ISBN 978-1-57916-158-3   An Answering Service Business
ISBN 978-1-57916-159-0   A Health Spa Business
ISBN 978-1-57916-160-6   A Restaurant Business
ISBN 978-1-57916-161-3   A Specialty Food Store Business
ISBN 978-1-57916-162-0   A Welding Business
ISBN 978-1-57916-163-7   A Day Care Center Business
ISBN 978-1-57916-164-4   A Flower and Plant Store Business
ISBN 978-1-57916-165-1   A Construction Electrician Business
ISBN 978-1-57916-166-8   A Housecleaning Service Business
ISBN 978-1-57916-167-5   A Nursing Service Business
ISBN 978-1-57916-168-2   A Bookkeeping Service Business
ISBN 978-1-57916-169-9   A Bed and Breakfast Business
ISBN 978-1-57916-170-5   A Secretarial Service Business
ISBN 978-1-57916-171-2   An Energy Specialist Business
ISBN 978-1-57916-172-9   A Guard Service Business
ISBN 978-1-57916-173-6   A Software Design Business
ISBN 978-1-57916-174-3   An Air Conditioning & Heating Business
ISBN 978-1-57916-175-0   A Plumbing Service Business
ISBN 978-1-57916-176-7   A Sewing Service Business
ISBN 978-1-57916-177-4   A Carpentry Service Business
ISBN 978-1-57916-178-1   A Home Attendent Service Business
ISBN 978-1-57916-179-8   A Tree Service Business
ISBN 978-1-57916-180-4   A Dairy Farming Business
ISBN 978-1-57916-181-1   A Farm Equipment Repair Service Business
ISBN 978-1-57916-182-8   A Children's Clothing Store Business
ISBN 978-1-57916-183-5   A Women's Apparel Store
ISBN 978-1-57916-184-2   A Convenience Food Store Business
ISBN 978-1-57916-185-9   A Pest Control Service Business
ISBN 978-1-57916-186-6   A Printing Business
ISBN 978-1-57916-187-3   An Ice Cream Business
ISBN 978-1-57916-188-0   A Mail Order Business
ISBN 978-1-57916-189-7   A Bookstore Business
ISBN 978-1-57916-190-3   A Home Furnishing Business
ISBN 978-1-57916-191-0   A Retail Florist Business
ISBN 978-1-57916-192-7   A Radio-Television Repair Shop Business
ISBN 978-1-57916-193-4   A Dry Cleaning Business
ISBN 978-1-57916-194-1   A Hardware Store Business
ISBN 978-1-57916-195-8   A Marine Retailing Business
ISBN 978-1-57916-196-5   An Office Products Business
ISBN 978-1-57916-197-2   A Pharmacy Business
ISBN 978-1-57916-198-9   A Fish Farming Business
ISBN 978-1-57916-199-6   A Personal Referral Service Business
ISBN 978-1-57916-200-9   A Solar Energy Business
ISBN 978-1-57916-201-6   A Building Service Contracting Business
ISBN 978-1-57916-202-3   A Retail Decorating Products Business
ISBN 978-1-57916-203-0   A Sporting Goods Store Business
ISBN 978-1-57916-204-7   A Retail Grocery Store
ISBN 978-1-57916-205-4   A Cosmetology Business
ISBN 978-1-57916-206-1   A Franchised Business
ISBN 978-1-57916-207-8   An Electronics Industry Consulting Practice Business
ISBN 978-1-57916-208-5   An Independent Consulting Practice Business
ISBN 978-1-57916-209-2   An Independent Trucking Business
ISBN 978-1-57916-210-8   An Accounting Service Business
ISBN 978-1-57916-211-5   A Nursery Business
ISBN 978-1-57916-212-2   A Seminar Promotion Business

ISBN 978-1-57916-231-9   A Bar & Cocktail Lounge Business
ISBN 978-1-57916-214-6   A Wheelchair Transportation Business
ISBN 978-1-57916-215-3   A Fertilizer and Pesticide Business
ISBN 978-1-57916-216-0   A Desktop Publishing Business
ISBN 978-1-57916-217-7   A Crime Prevention Business
ISBN 978-1-57916-218-4   A Gift Shop Business
ISBN 978-1-57916-219-1   A Handcraft Success Business
ISBN 978-1-57916-220-7   A Coin-Operated Laundries Business
ISBN 978-1-57916-221-4   A Property Management Business
ISBN 978-1-57916-222-1   An Auto Supply Store Business
ISBN 978-1-57916-223-8   A Men's Apparel Store Business
ISBN 978-1-57916-224-5   A Temporary Help Service Business
ISBN 978-1-57916-225-2   An Advertising Agency Business
ISBN 978-1-57916-226-9   A Firewood Sales Business
ISBN 978-1-57916-227-6   A Children's Bookstore Business
ISBN 978-1-57916-228-3   A Used Bookstore Business
ISBN 978-1-57916-229-0   A Sandwich Shop Deli Business
ISBN 978-1-57916-230-6   An Instant Print/Copy Shop
ISBN 978-1-57916-231-3   A Gift Specialty Store Business
ISBN 978-1-57916-232-0   A Gift Basket Service Business
ISBN 978-1-57916-233-7   A Hospitality Management Business
ISBN 978-1-57916-234-4   A Hotel Business
ISBN 978-1-57916-235-1   A Catering Service Business
ISBN 978-1-57916-236-8   A Carpet-Cleaning Service Business
ISBN 978-1-57916-237-5   A Window-Washing Service Business
ISBN 978-1-57916-238-2   An Innkeeping Service Business
ISBN 978-1-57916-239-9   An Apartment Preparation Service
ISBN 978-1-57916-240-5   A Kiosks and Cart Business
ISBN 978-1-57916-241-2   A Janitorial Service Business
ISBN 978-1-57916-242-9   A Medical Claims Processing Business
ISBN 978-1-57916-243-6   A Nursing Home Care Business
ISBN 978-1-57916-244-3   A Home Health Care Business
ISBN 978-1-57916-245-0   A Referral Services Business
ISBN 978-1-57916-246-7   A Hair Styling Salon Business
ISBN 978-1-57916-247-4   A Child Care Service Business

How-To Business Books

ISBN 978-1-57916-248-1   How to Buy and Sell A Business
ISBN 978-1-57916-249-8   How to Advertise A Small Business
ISBN 978-1-57916-250-4   How to Write A Successful Business Plan
ISBN 978-1-57916-251-1   How to Finance Your Business for the 21st Century
ISBN 978-1-57916-252-8   How to Market Your Business for the 21st Century
ISBN 978-1-57916-152-1   How to Start & Manage Your Own Business
ISBN 978-1-57916-152-1   How to Start & Manage a Home Based Business
ISBN 978-1-57916-152-1   How to Start a Participative Management Program

To Order Business Plans

Please Remit To:
    Lewis & Renn Associates
    10315 Harmony Drive
    Interlochen, Michigan 49643

ISBN # _____ Title _____

ISBN # _____ Title _____

Name _____

Address _____

City _____

State _____ Zip _____

Business Book _____

U.S. Shipping & Postage   **$ 3.00**

Total _____

Library Discount - 20%
Retail Discount - 20%
$3.00 Postage & Handling
$21.95 Each
www.smallbusbooks.com